KAIROS
MOMENTS
WORKBOOK

By Denise Sherriff
with
Nellie Keasling

Edited by the HGR Editorial Services
Homer G. Rhea, Editor
Nellie Keasling, Copy Editor
Lonna Gattenby, Layout and Cover Design
homer8238@gmail.com

ISBN: 978-1-0895564-0-4

Printed by Derek Press
Cleveland, Tennessee 37311
United States of America

Table of Contents

Guidelines

This workbook is written to be a study aid for the student of *Kairos Moments*, a book written by Denise Sherriff. The workbook has one worksheet per chapter. The worksheet will contain the following information:

1. **Fill in the blanks:**

   These are taken directly from the chapters. However, if for some reason you need to check your answers, an answer key is provided at the end of the workbook.

2. **Discussion Questions:**

   The discussion questions are designed to help you think about the important themes, metaphors, and thoughts of the author given in the chapter. Please think about your answers and listen as others in the group share their thoughts. Sharing thoughts helps people to broaden their thinking and analyze their thoughts. Be open to what others are saying.

3. **Group Activity:**

   This section is designed to help you apply what you have learned. As you work with others in your group, you will hear how they would respond to a situation. Together, you can come to a decision on the best way to answer the situation or pray for a solution. Be open to hearing what God has to say to you in your heart or in the Bible as you work through a scenario or answer a thought-provoking question.

4. **Digging Deeper:**

   These questions are designed for you individually to search your heart and your Bible as you ask God for wisdom. Some of the questions can be discussed in the class if the instructor desires to do so.

Some of the group activities will require looking up words and scriptures in the Bible. You will need a Bible with a concordance in the back or Bible Gateway App on your Smart phone. (Bible Gateway is a free app.)

Workbook

Chapter 1
The Opportunity of Offense

Fill in the Blank:

1. We all have the same opportunity anyone else has to rise above any hurt, _____, _____, or _____.

2. Know who you are in Christ, and be _____ toward others.

3. He loves to put each of us on the _____ _____ and give us a spin.

4. God is emphatically capable of doing a _____ and _____ restoration in you; however, He may choose not to.

5. Your journey is a _____.

Discussion Questions:

1. Why do you think the author uses several figures of speech? (For example, "like a car stuck in the mud.")

2. Find at least two other figures of speech in this first chapter and explain the importance of their use in context of the paragraph.

3. What does the author mean in her title about "the opportunity of offense"? Explain your perception of this title.

Group Activity:

Divide into groups of three or four. Allow the participants in the group a few minutes to share a personal experience of offense, abuse, or criticism they have endured. Allow them to explain how they responded to this offense. Was it an opportunity or a misfortune? Could this offense have been handled differently? How?

Digging Deeper:

1. What do you think the author means by "God putting us on the Potter's wheel and giving us a spin"? Explain this concept taken from Jeremiah 18. Has this ever happened to you?

2. Explain what you think the author means about a believer's journey being a process.

3. The author says, "His help is on the way to restoring you." She gives two Bible verses that support her claim. Find at least two more verses that you think support the claim that God's help is yours.

Chapter 2

<h1 align="center">Demolition Crew</h1>

Fill in the Blank:

1. The dismantling of a building gives a glimpse of what it's like to be totally undone by_____, so a new thing can _____.

2. When dismantled, it's the end of this building, but the _____.

3. God's people are not _____.

4. If problems are covered up, there's always a chance they_____.

Discussion Questions:

1. Discuss the metaphor of the demolition of a building from dismantling to disposal.

2. What do you think the author meant by the following statement? "Everything has a measure of life in it, and not everything is used up when it appears to be expired." Give an example of how this statement might be true.

3. How does the author relate the demolition of a building to the spiritual side of the believer?

Group Activity:

Ask the group if they have watched a house or building demolition. (Some may have actually been on the site of a demolition.) Discuss what came out of the old house and how they disposed of the old materials. Was anything recycled or repurposed? Why? What did they do to make it new again? How can this be compared to an individual's life?

Digging Deeper:

1. What do you think the author meant by saying, "God's people are not 'throwaways'"?

2. The author mentions the refining and testing process. What does this process involve when referring to silver? (Check the Internet to read about the process.)What are the spiritual implications of this process?

3. What does a "brand new you" look like?

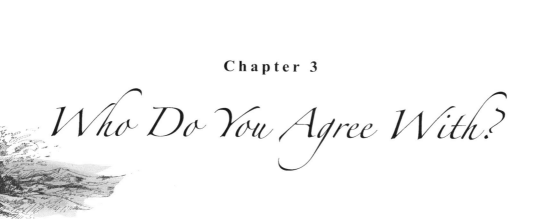

Chapter 3

Who Do You Agree With?

Fill in the Blank:

1. Satan knocks at our door with an enticing agenda of _____.

2. We're aware of our Enemy's _____ _____.

3. The package Satan leaves at our door represents a _____ _____.

4. Be watchful of your own eyes; equip yourself with _____ _____.

Discussion Questions:

1. Explain the metaphor of Satan knocking at the door and the package he leaves.

2. Explain looking through "rose-colored glasses." Why is this dangerous?

3. How does the saying, "curiosity killed the cat" entice us to explore the "package" left at our doorstep? Explain the spiritual implications.

4. If you were visibly face-to-face with Satan (as Jesus was in His temptation in the wilderness), how would you resist the "beauty and secret opportunity" offered to you?

Group Activity:

As a group, read Matthew 4:1-11 about Jesus' temptation in the wilderness. Discuss the following:

1. Why did the devil tempt Jesus to turn stones into bread? Are you ever tempted by food? How can you resist the temptation?

2. In the temptation to jump off a high building, what human need is at the heart of this temptation? Are you ever tempted in this way? Give an example.

3. Are you ever tempted to worship something other than God? Give examples and tell how you resist the temptation. Does having idols carry the same weight as worshiping Satan? Explain.

Digging Deeper:

1. Regarding lust, Job said: "I have made a covenant with my eyes" (Job 31:1). How does this line up with what Jesus said in Matthew 5:28? Does this apply to Christians today? Explain what happens if a believer succumbs to temptation of this kind?

2. The author exhorts her readers to "Be watchful of your own eyes, and equip yourself with God's view." Then, she makes several statements resisting Satan. Add three statements of your own, resisting Satan's temptations.

Chapter 4

Be of Sound Mind and Body

Fill in the Blank:

1. A healthy body plus a healthy mind equal _____ _____.

2. _____ _____ strengthens our body and mind.

3. The Holy Bible is the _____ of our lives.

4. Welcoming a (an) _____ lifestyle is exactly what [we] should do.

Discussion Questions:

1. The author says, "Cookies and milk are delicious, but a diet of this alone won't get the job done." Explain this statement in the physical, and then draw the comparison to the spiritual life.

2. The author says, "The Holy Bible is the almanac of our lives." Explain the metaphor of the almanac.

3. When referring to "well-rounded fitness," the author says she has to be the one to bring about the necessary changes; therefore, she has to define "better options." Suggest some of the options which might bring about "well-rounded fitness." Does this mean in the physical realm only? Explain.

Group Activity:

Perhaps someone in your group knows somebody who has once battled alcohol or drugs. Ask the individual if he/she will come and talk to your group about the struggle he/she had when tempted to take the first drink, first smoke, or first drug. Once addicted, how did this individual overcome the addiction? Read Romans 7:23 and compare what Paul says to what this person described in the testimony. How does Paul recommend resolving this conflict between the body and the mind? Explain why accountability is important to someone trying to overcome a problem.

Digging Deeper:

1. Write a personal essay describing your own struggles of the flesh. What have you done to overcome these struggles? Write down scripture references, songs, poems, or advice from someone who has helped you with these times of weaknesses. Save this essay and use it as a testimony when the time is right.

C h a p t e r   5

Pictures Are Worth a Thousand Emotions

Fill in the Blank:

1.   The eyes see our world _____; our heart sees through _____.

2.   Excellence is not perfection. Excellence means _____ _____.

3.   It takes _____to discover what NOT to do.

4.   Keep your dreams alive by engaging your _____.

Discussion Questions:

1.   When looking at a photograph, can one see more than what is depicted in the photo? How? What can be seen?

2.   How can parents' love for their children compare to God's love for His children? Use scripture verses to substantiate your comparisons.

3.   What does the author mean by her statement: "Like any good inventor, it takes mistakes to discover what NOT to do"?

4.   What does the author say we want for our children, and how do we accomplish it?

Group Activity:

Ask someone to read aloud the synopsis about Thomas Edison, the inventor of the light bulb.

•   Talk about how you would have felt after failing to invent something numerous times.

•   Talk about the author's statement: "It takes mistakes to discover what NOT to do."

•   What are you going to take away from the story of Thomas Edison and the author's statement in this lesson?

Digging Deeper:

1. In Ephesians 6:4, Paul writes: "And you fathers, do not provoke your children to wrath, but bring them up in the training and admonition of the Lord" (NKJV). The Message version says, "Fathers, don't exasperate your children by coming down hard on them. Take them by the hand and lead them in the way of the Master."

   • What emotions do you feel when you consider this verse?

   • Why do you think Paul addressed this verse to the "fathers"?

   • In general, do fathers lead their families "in the way of the Master"?

   • How did your dad "lead" your family?

   • How are you leading your family?

Chapter 5
Story
Thomas Edison, the Inventor

Thomas Edison's teachers said he was "too stupid to learn anything." He was fired from his first two jobs for being "non-productive." As an inventor, Edison made 1,000 unsuccessful attempts of inventing the light bulb.

"Many of life's failures," the supreme innovator said, "are people who did not realize how close they were to success when they gave up." Before that magical moment in October 1879, Edison had worked out no fewer than 3,000 theories about electric light, each of them reasonable and apparently likely to be true—but in only two cases did his experiments work.

No one likes failure, but the smart innovators learn from it. Mark Gumz, the head of Olympus America, attributes some of the company's successes in diagnostic technology to understanding failure and acting on the knowledge. His mantra: "You only fail when you quit."

The striking thing about the innovators who succeeded in making our modern world is how often they failed. Turn on a light, take a photograph, watch television, search the Web, jet across the Pacific, or talk on a cell phone. The innovators who left us such legacies had to find the way to Eldorado* through a maze of wrong turns.

*Eldorado is a legendary country in South America which is supposed to be rich in gold and precious stones. Eldorado was sought by early Spanish explorers.

Oh, the Joy of Parenting

Fill in the Blank:

1. The author says her "job [is] _____ _____ or a _____ __ ____ _____."

2. "I'm thankful for windows of _____."

3. "The number of children we have doesn't dictate the level of _____."

4. "Love through all things and all years with your_____."

Discussion Questions:

1. Should moms stay at home with their children? Why?

2. What are some things the author listed in which she took pleasure when her child was small? Then, she comments that suddenly the child is saying, "Oh mom, I can't wear that." What does this really tell us about rearing children?

3. What are some of the rewards of instilling good values, time-tested teachings, and biblical principles to children as they grow up in the home?

4. Why do you think the author included the following verse at the end of this chapter?

   "Let my teaching drop as the rain, My speech distill as the dew, as raindrops on the tender herb, and as showers on the grass" (Deuteronomy 32:2 NKJV).

Group Activity:

Ask several people in your group to relate a story about a special occasion in their childhood which was made outstanding by something their parents did for them. For example, one might remember a special Christmas, birthday, school play, or helping someone in need. Ask the person why this has been so special for them that they still remember it.

Digging Deeper:

1. Why do you think parents, especially in biblical times, wanted children badly enough to plead with God for them? Is this still true today? Give some examples.

2. What is our worth to God? Give examples from Scripture.

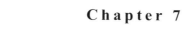

Chapter 7

Fill in the Blank:

1. Creativity is _____.

2. When God speaks a Word, there are usually two things that happen:

   (1) _____ the Word.

   (2) Doing the _____ that follows.

3. We have no idea what one person can accomplish when he/she gets in touch with the _____ God has given.

4. Fully _____ the _____ of creativity that you can have in Christ.

Discussion Questions:

1. How do we know when God speaks a "word" to us?

2. Explain how creativity and freedom work together.

3. The author says that the Enemy will try to pervert the word God has spoken. Why? Do we always realize when Satan is trying to trip us up or set a trap for us? How do we fight against the devil so God's action can be carried out?

4. The author says to "create something incredible." Give some examples of something incredible you have created at the prompting of the Holy Spirit.

Group Activity:

Break up into groups of two or three. Decide on a creative project that you can volunteer to do in your community to help the needy. Visit Habitat for Humanity, a soup kitchen, the Salvation Army, or some other organization in your community. Find out what they need and help supply that need.

Digging Deeper:

1. Give three biblical examples of someone who accomplished a task given to them by God.

2. Think back over your life. How has God led you through difficult circumstances to where you are today? Can you see where God directed you to do something for Him? Give examples.

Chapter 8

The Arborist

Fill in the Blank:

1. Seasons of birth and death alike inspire _____.

2. The tree is an example of how God _____ us.

3. Springtime "springs" forth brilliantly because of the process of _____ in winter.

4. His Word removes _____ _____ from our lives, so we can maintain _____, _____ in promotion of His kingdom.

Discussion Questions:

1. The author uses the metaphor of the tree with its seasons of life and death. Compare this metaphor to people and their seasons of life. Now, discuss the spiritual implications of this comparison.

2. The author described the process of pruning a tree. How does this compare to the believer's spiritual life?

3. Read Psalm 1:3, and explain the comparison of the tree planted by the water and the believer.

Group Activity:

Ask the group how to grow a tree. After listing what they think is important, go to the Internet and select a site that explains how to grow a tree. Note the process of growing a tree, including the pruning. With this knowledge, draw a comparison to your own spiritual growth. Include in your comparison, the right soil, growing conditions, pruning, etc.

Digging Deeper:

1. Read Luke 13:6-8: The owner of the fig tree asked Jesus not to destroy the tree because it was not producing fruit. The owner proposed to care for the tree another year before destroying it. How does this parable of the fig tree compare to the believer's life? What is the believer's fruit? Will a believer be destroyed if he/she does not produce "fruit"? Explain your view on this.

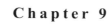

Chapter 9

That Is So Irritating!

Fill in the Blank:

1. What do we do when something _____ us?

2. One of the things the Bible says about animals, birds, insects, etc. is that we have _____ over them.

3. Pertaining to people though, these are my _____ in Christ. I do not have _____ over them.

4. Find the gift of _____ within you.

Discussion Questions:

1. When something gets on your nerves, how do you react? Why?

2. As a believer in Christ, how should we respond to irritating circumstances? Give some examples.

3. What does the word *forbearance* mean? What does the Bible say about forbearance?

4. How did God mean for us "to have dominion" over the animal kingdom? Give examples.

Group Activity:

Divide into smaller groups of three or four. Give the groups the following scenario to discuss:

> You work in a large office which has one big room divided into cubicles for the office workers. You need to concentrate on your job, but it is difficult when some of your coworkers are humming, smacking and popping gum, clipping their fingernails (some of the clippings even landed on your desk), and sighing loudly.

Since you are a Christ-follower, how can you maintain your sanity and still be a witness to your coworkers? Give several suggestions how to deal with these irritants.

Digging Deeper:

1. Research on the Internet how a pearl is formed. It all starts with an irritant.

   How does this story compare to dealing with irritants in your life? Do you always have good results after solving the problematic irritant?

2. What are the rewards of a peacemaker? Back up your answers with scripture references.

C h a p t e r 1 0

You're Made the Way You're Made

Fill in the Blank:

1. Each of us is uniquely made with _____.

2. This is not about pride. It's about our unique gifts, _____, and _____ that make us distinctive.

3. When we view others as gifted in their respective ways, we _____ one another.

4. If we spend too much time trying to improve in areas just to be like someone else, it's highly possible that our unique qualities will become _____.

Discussion Questions:

1. What are your gifts and talents? Why do you think God gave you the ones you have? Is it wrong to wish for talents like someone else? Why?

2. How do we improve our areas of weakness?

3. If we ask God to show us what He sees when He looks at us, what can we expect to happen?

4. What is the author referring to in the last paragraph when she says, "Sprinkle some bling"?

5. What is your purpose in life?

Group Activity:

Ask someone in the group to go to the Internet and look up "Fun Facts About the Human Body."

Read aloud the results to the entire group. Now ask the group to read the following verses:

Psalm 139:13-16; Jeremiah 1:5; Genesis 1:27.

With these scriptures and facts in mind, how should we live our lives? What are some adjectives that would describe your feelings toward God and others?

Digging Deeper:

1. In Psalm 139:14, David said, "We are fearfully and wonderfully made." Explain how this is true. Is this statement true for those who are born deformed or handicapped? Explain.

2. Read Romans 12:4-8 NIV; 1 Corinthians 12 NKJV. Thinking about your own church congregation, how many gifts of the Spirit are operating in your church? How are these operating gifts like one body? Is your church body complete? If some of the gifts are missing, how would the completion of the gifts help your church?

Adornment

Fill in the Blank:

1. When we worship the Lord, we are, in a sense, decorating ourselves with an enrichment of _____that honors Him with _____.

2. What are we wearing in the spirit to represent and glorify God? Are we embracing _____that shows honor, and when released, brings _____to others?

3. By which _____are we trying to measure ourselves?

4. Beauty is a reflection of a healthier life. It's a life that exudes wellness and is accented with the _____ _____ _____ _____.

Discussion Questions:

1. Describe the difference between adoration of praise and the adornment of jewelry.

2. Why do you think the author wants us to ask ourselves: *By which standards should we measure ourselves?*

3. What does beauty reflect in us?

4. Do people know if believers are reflecting the fruit of the Spirit? How?

Group Activity and Digging Deeper:

1. As a group, discuss how Christians wear different masks. Name some masks Christians wear. What are they trying to hide?

2. Discuss how Christians are supposed to adorn their bodies. (Note the author's first paragraph and last paragraph on page 21.)

   • Is the author referring to the physical adornment, spiritual adornment, or both?

- How are God's people supposed to dress to honor God? Use scriptures to back up your answer.

- Since God looks on the heart instead of the outward appearance (1 Samuel 16:7), does it matter how we dress? Why?

Chapter 12

The Resistance

Fill in the Blank:

1. Suddenly and exactly when we need it, God reveals a _____ to us.

2. Stir up _____ and _____ for what God says you can do, because He has prepared the way and will meet you there.

3. Don't be afraid to take aim and commit yourself to a challenge, because there is a will of _____ in you.

4. _____ is crucial to what and how our opposition operates.

5. The exercise of _____ fortifies our physical and spiritual selves.

Discussion Questions:

1. In 1 Samuel 17:48, the story says that David ran toward his opposition (the giant). How was David able to do this? Is this the same precedent believers are to follow when battling Satan? Give scripture references to back up your answer.

2. How do we resist the devil?

3. According to the author, "discernment is crucial to what and how our opposition operates." Explain this statement.

4. How is the physical and the spiritual resistance complementary to one another?

Group Activity:

Ask the group if they can think of situations in the Bible where the Enemy waged war against a person serving God. Make a list of these stories. Now, discuss how the individual in the Bible stories fought against Satan and became victorious.

When we are in a crisis where Satan is attacking us, what is an effective weapon to use against him?

Digging Deeper:

1. Read about the Christian soldier's armor in Ephesians 6:13-17. How do we use the sword of the Spirit—the Word of God—against the devil? Give examples.

2. Go to the Website *www.wikihow.com/Mentally-Prepare-Soldiers-for-the-Stress-of-Warfare* and read how soldiers are prepared by the military to go to war. Near the end of the article, there are eight tips and three warnings. Rewrite the three warnings for the believer who is fighting against "the rulers of the darkness of this age" (Ephesians 6:12).

Chapter 13

Why Bless God?

Fill in the Blank:

1. What could we possibly do that would _____ [God]?

2. We are not to set ourselves above others as though they are not worthy of _____ and _____.

3. _____ blesses God.

4. _____ is the connection between God and man.

Discussion Questions:

1. In your opinion, what does it mean to "bless God"?

2. What does the author mean when she says, "behavior blesses God"?

3. How is "godliness" the connection between God and man?

4. Answer the question, "Why Bless God"?

Group Activity:

Ask someone in the group to read Psalm 103:1-5. David is blessing God for various things which God has done for him.

Ask the group to contribute words describing blessings from God which they have experienced. When all the contributions are written down, ask the group to try to use them in a rhyming pattern. Rhyming words help our memory.

37 | *The Opportunity of Offense*

Digging Deeper:

1. The author, in her last paragraph, suggests that we should consider ministering to ourselves. What does this mean? Are there examples in the Bible of this? If so, jot down the occasions and Scripture references.

2. Play some worship music softly in the background, and practice "blessing God." Write down in a diary or journal how you felt doing this spiritual exercise.

C h a p t e r   1 4

Prayer Is Serious Business

Fill in the Blank:

1. Prayer affects _____ in us and our _____.

2. A _____ _____ is also known as the "Jesus Prayer" or "Prayer of the Heart."

3. Depending upon what needs have touched your heart is what determines your _____ ____ _____.

4. Prayer _____ our relationships and prayer should never be _____.

Discussion Questions:

1. Does it matter to God what position we are in when praying (kneeling, standing, sitting)? Support your answer with Scripture.

2. The author suggests praying a "breath prayer." What does this mean? Is this something we should practice? Why?

3. Are there differences in prayer; for example, praying for a child's sick pet or praying for a loved one undergoing heart surgery?

4. Does God answer all prayers? Support your answer with Scripture.

Group Activity:

Have a testimony time where everybody gives a testimony of answered prayer in no more than two minutes. (This can be done in "popcorn" fashion. As soon as one person finishes, another person stands up and gives testimony, until everyone has participated.)

Digging Deeper:

1. List all the kinds of prayers you can think of and explain them. For example, the Sinner's Prayer is prayed when someone needs to accept Christ as his/her Savior.

2. Research to find out what the Prayer of Relinquishment is and explain it.

3. Where in the Bible are Christ's prayers? List them.

Chapter 15

I Don't Need Discipline; I'm Always Right

Fill in the Blank:

1. Note this formula: Knowledge + _____ + accountability = _____.

2. Plenty of people are watching us while our lives are in _____ _____.

3. Walk in _____.

4. Our lives have a myriad of _____. Each one prepares us for the next.

Discussion Questions:

1. What attitude shows in the title of this lesson?

2. Explain why we need accountability in our lives.

3. Expound on the comparison the author gives of instruction from the Bible and a road map. If the instructions from the Bible and the road map are incomplete or faulty, what are the consequences?

4. What does the Bible say about humility? Why is it hard to be humble?

Group Activity:

Divide into groups of three or four. Ask the groups to write a blog on how to be humble. List Scripture references dealing with humility and the sin of pride.

Hint: You may want to start with a scripture verse or a quote and use it for a springboard to write your blog.

Ask someone from each group to read the group's blog to the rest of the group.

Digging Deeper:

1. Research the Scriptures to find out what Jesus had to say about humility.

2. Go to the Internet and find quotes on humility. (Example: "Being humble means that we are not on earth to see how important we can become, but to see how much difference we can make in the lives of others."—Gordon B. Hinckley)

Find a quote you really like and display it on your desk at work.

Chapter 16

Craving You, Lord, Is Fleeting; Greater That I Desire You

Fill in the Blank:

1. When we have desire, it's mostly for something we perceive as _____.

2. The Word tells us we are to desire the _____ ____ _____.

3. _____ is a temporary want that will soon diminish.

4. Desire is lasting and lives in the deepest recesses of our _____ and _____.

Discussion Questions:

1. Explain the difference in *craving* and *desire*. Give an example.

2. How do individuals become aware of what is good or bad for them? Are there gray areas in our desires? Give examples.

3. Explain the author's question in paragraph three: "How vested am I in travailing for what I know is most excellent for me and will turn my craving into desire?"

4. How does one get to the place where there is a deep desire (longing) for a closeness with God?

Group Activity:

1. Ask someone to read David's Psalm 63:1-8 in the NKJV aloud to the group. Analyze the verses. Make notes about their meaning. Now, ask someone to read the same passage from the *Message* Bible.

2. Which verse of this psalm best fits your relationship with God? Why?

3. How might you deepen your first love with God?

Digging Deeper:

Do a word study on the words "crave" and "desire." What are the differences? Does Jesus address the theme of desiring things of God? Where in the Bible? What does Paul have to say about the same theme? After doing the word study, what is your conclusion?

No Such Thing as Buying More Time

Fill in the Blank:

1. At some time, we have all wanted to somehow acquire more _____.

2. There is no way to pay back time; it's _____ _____.

3. The best we can hope for is to _____ what we have.

4. Our goal is to be _____.

Discussion Questions:

1. Why do you think we need more time in a 24-hour day? Give several reasons.

2. Discuss the scenario where Joshua commanded the sun to stand still in the heavens (Joshua 10:12). Do you think God would do something like that today? Why?

3. The author says our "goal is to be liberated." What does she mean by this statement?

4. What is the best way to manage your time?

Group Activity:

Reread paragraph three in the lesson. The author asks you to prioritize your daily activities and assign a value from 0 to 10. Together, come up with a list of activities for one week. Some examples might be: job; going to church; Bible study; prayer time; laundry; cooking; cleaning, etc. Assign a value to each item. Now, prioritize them from 0 to 10, with 10 being the highest.

Next, figure how many hours in a week and how much time you spend on each of your items, including sleep time per week. For example, you spend 40 hours per week on your job. How much time do you spend in church, etc.? Do you have time left over?

Digging Deeper:

1. Considering the group activity, how much time do you personally spend on these activities? How much time in Bible study and prayer; how much time with your family, etc.?

2. How can you reduce your time spent on things that are perhaps not as important as others, such as TV and social media? Give some suggestions.

Chapter 18

What's on Your Schedule Today?

Fill in the Blank:

1. Spending time with God does not necessarily need to be _____.

2. Remember to _____.

3. He [God] is better than a _____ _____.

4. _____ is a process of relating.

Discussion Questions:

1. The author says we do not have to have a planned time with God. God is everywhere all the time. This is true; however, what are the benefits of having a set prayer time and Bible study with God every day?

2. The author urges us not to forget to listen. Does God speak to you? When? How?

3. How is God better than a "best friend"?

4. Is anything too insignificant to pray about? Can we pray about anything; for example, asking God for a good parking space at the Mall? Why would God want to answer that kind of prayer when so much suffering is going on in the world?

Group Activity:

The Bible says in Revelation 12:11 we are overcomers by the "blood of the Lamb and the word of [our] testimony." So, ask the group to share about a time when they prayed at an unscheduled time. Did God hear them and answer their prayer?

Digging Deeper:

1. Did Jesus schedule time to pray to His heavenly Father? Give Scripture references.

2. Did Jesus pray at unscheduled times? Give Scripture references.

Chapter 19

Who We Are and Who We Are Not

Fill in the Blank:

1. God's desire for us is to be_____.

2. When I go to the altar, I practice leaving my _____there.

3. I remember to make an _____with God.

4. I do not leave the altar without taking His _____with me.

Discussion Questions:

1. Explain how God knows who we are and who we are not.

2. The author says we can make an exchange with God. What does she mean?

3. Explain the following statement: "Unravel your cares and be completely 'undone' at the altar."

4. Does God expect us to pray for our leaders, even if we do not agree or like them? Use Scripture references to support your answer.

Group Activity:

Divide into groups of three or four. Ask each member of the group to tell one thing the others do not know about you. Tell each other what your goal is in life. How far along the way are you to accomplishing this goal? Now, join hands and pray for each other to make an exchange of hindrances for the joy of the Lord.

Digging Deeper:

1. Make a list of things in your life you are bringing to the altar to leave in exchange for God's comfort and gladness. This, of course, will be done in the privacy of your home.

2. Read Isaiah 61:3; write down how this verse applies to you.

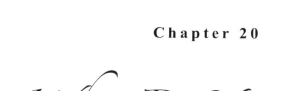

What Do Your Words Actually Say?

Fill in the Blank:

1. Just as truth matters, so does the way we address others and the _____ ____ _____ we use.

2. We don't hear how we sound to _____ in the same way they hear _____.

3. One of the most constructive helps is to take _____ captive before speaking.

4. We must reflect Christ, by speaking in ways that can be heard as _____ toward excellence.

Discussion Questions:

1. Why does the author say she appreciates what is being said to her to be trustworthy?

2. Why is tone of voice important when speaking to others? Explain.

3. What is the difference in the tone of voice Jesus used when He rebuked the Pharisees, saying, "Woe to you . . . for you are full of hypocrisy and lawlessness"; than when he told the woman taken in adultery, "Neither do I condemn you, go and sin no more."

4. Should ministers be aware of their tone of voice used in the pulpit? If so, what should be their tone of voice? Explain.

Group Activity:

Read the story on the next page.

Ask several members of the group to volunteer to participate in an activity. Ask two different people to say the same phrase in a different way.

1. "I love you" (sarcastically).
2. "I love you" (sincerely).

1. "You need to pay your tithes!" (Emphatically)
2. "You need to pay your tithes!" (Lovingly)

The instructor may want to suggest other examples.

Digging Deeper:

Luke wrote in 12:12: "For the Holy Spirit will teach you in that very hour what you ought to say." Find another scripture verse that deals with speaking and tone of voice.

How do you want others to hear you speaking? Why?

Chapter 20

Story

The Farmer Who Couldn't Read

The story was told about a country farmer who couldn't read. His son went away to college to better himself. One day the farmer received a letter from his son. So, the farmer took it to a neighbor and asked him to read it to him.

The neighbor's gruff voice read: "DEAR DAD, I NEED MONEY! COULD YOU PLEASE SEND ME SOME MONEY BY NEXT WEEK?"

The farmer said, "I'm not sending him a penny. He can get a job and go to work."

Not satisfied, however, the farmer took the letter to another neighbor and asked him to read it.

This neighbor with a soft-spoken, kind voice read: "Dear Dad, I need money. Could you please send me some money by next week?"

The farmer said, "Of course, I'll send him some money. He's trying to better himself."

—Anonymous

Chapter 21

I Will Not Be Moved

Fill in the Blank:

1. _____ act as an anchor that give trees steadiness.

2. Much goes on _____ to take care of what goes on _____.

3. One of the most determining factors is the _____.

4. Strength needs to reside with _____ so we do not collapse.

Discussion Questions:

1. Explain which weather conditions are better for trees to grow and maintain their stability.

2. Name several weather conditions and decide which is the most important for the strength of a tree?

3. Why is wind important to keeping a tree stabilized?

4. Compare this lesson to one's spiritual condition.

Group Activity:

Have someone research the palm tree on the Internet, and then read about how its root system keeps it from being destroyed during hurricanes. Share the information with the group.

Explain the metaphor of the tree; for example, the roots are what? The trunk is what? etc.

Compare the palm tree to the believer in Christ. What are the similarities? How does one become anchored? Write your comparison on the worksheet for Chapter 21. Also, find verses in the Bible that talk about the palm tree, and write these references on the worksheet.

Digging Deeper:

1. What things might create a "hurricane" in a believer's life?

2. What can believers do to avoid catastrophe when the storms of life come?

3. Find several verses in the Bible that talk about trees and their stability.

Worksheet

Palm Tree

BRANCHES AND LEAVES (Fronds)

TRUNK

ROOTS

The roots of a palm tree are fibrous; they not only spread out to great distances, but also go down deep. So, all this combines to give a palm tree a very solid base in the ground. The trunk is supple which will allow it to bend in the wind without breaking.

Chapter 22

Unexpected Surprise

Fill in the Blank:

1. With the blessing of children in our lives, we must expect the _____.

2. Life does not happen without unplanned _____.

3. God has entrusted our children to our_____.

4. God's borders allow for mistakes, growing, learning, _____, and _____ that develop character and personality.

Discussion Questions:

1. When the unimaginable happens, it catches us off guard. What is the best way to handle unexpected situations?

2. The author says, "Life does not happen without unplanned upsets." So with that in mind, is there anything we can do to prepare for future upsets?

3. Why do you think it is that children bring many of these unexpected events?

4. Since we are God's children, do we bring unexpected situations to Him? Or . . . is it unexpected to God?

Group Activity:

Divide into groups of two or three. Give them one of the following unexpected situations to deal with.

- You are a graduate student, and during an examination, you discover you do not know the answers.

- You are leaving for work when you suddenly discover a leak in the kitchen water pipe.

- You lose your home and all your possessions in a fire.

- You lose someone you love to cancer.

As a group, decide how to handle this situation. Come up with an alternate plan, in case the first one doesn't work.

Digging Deeper:

Are we responsible before God for unexpected situations our children create? Support your answer with Scripture.

Chapter 23

People Watchers

Fill in the Blank:

1. If you sit in a judgment seat, it's usually a combination of a situation and _____.

2. The Enemy always uses people to _____ others.

3. Where assessment and evaluation walk without discernment, it's called _____ _____.

4. _____ weighs a great deal when we have it thrust upon us.

Discussion Questions:

1. What is wrong with "people watching"? Give examples.

2. Is the following statement true? "We oftentimes misunderstand what we don't understand." Explain. Give examples.

3. What are the Enemy's tactics to break up relationships and hurt others? How can the Enemy be stopped? Give scripture references to support your answer.

4. In what way does 1 Timothy 5:13 support this lesson?

Group Activity:

Divide into groups of three or four. Ask the groups to look at the pictures of people on the next page. Do not look at the people critically. Choose at least three people and write down something positive about the people you chose. These are people Jesus died for and people who perhaps need salvation. Ask each group how hard it was to say something positive. Why is it hard to be positive? Remember to pray for the people you see in the mall, at Walmart, or the pharmacy.

Digging Deeper:

Go to the Internet and find the lyrics to the song, "People Need the Lord." Read these lyrics and ask the Lord what he wants you to do about the people who pass you every day on the street or in the mall or in the grocery store. Ask the Lord to give you compassion for the lost.

Worksheet

People Watchers

People at the Mall

www.alamy.com - B6J6WW

People in Russia

Chapter 24

I Have a Stomachache

Fill in the Blank:

1. We have to choose _____.

2. We don't _____ take specific _____ over our mind and thoughts like we should.

3. Go to God in prayer instead of the _____.

4. God is stirring you to _____ _____ the very thing He has placed within you.

Discussion Questions:

1. Explain what you think the author meant when she said, "There is an ache . . . deep within your belly."

2. Have you ever experienced this sensation? Where did it lead? Did you pray about it? How was the experience resolved?

3. What is the spiritual analogy to the "ache"?

Group Activity:

Ask your group to look up the definitions to the following words:

1. Discernment   3. Apprehension
2. Intuition   4. Uneasiness

How do you think these words play into this lesson? If we experience apprehension, intuition, or uneasiness, how does discernment help?

When are we likely to experience the "ache" in our belly which the author describes? How would you solve it?

Digging Deeper:

1. What does the Bible say about being *anxious*? Look up scriptures on the word anxious, and write down the reference. Summarize the meaning.

2. What does the Bible say about *discernment*? Look up scriptures on the word discern, and write down the reference. Summarize the meaning.

3. What is God saying to you about being anxious?

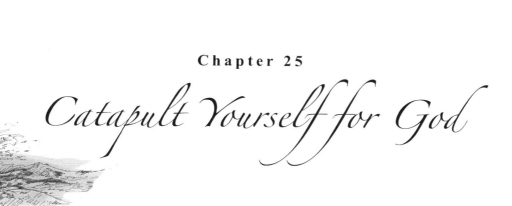

Chapter 25

Catapult Yourself for God

Fill in the Blank:

1. Once you're out in the deep for God, then you're out in the deep _____God.

2. The _____ was used to launch any number of objects for both defense and attack.

3. Most of us . . . take our _____ ___ _____ one at a time.

4. Our entire path is a school of learning that compels us _____.

Discussion Questions:

1. Give a brief history of the catapult. Is there a modern-day catapult?

2. Why do most people take cautious steps in doing something, rather than being catapulted into action?

3. Is there a place in our lives for the catapult? Explain.

4. Explain the title of this lesson.

Group Activity:

On the next page, look at the pictures of the catapult. Go to the Internet and look it up. Read about its construction and uses. Also, find out what kind of destruction the catapult made. Is some form of this device used today? If we catapult ourselves into God's service, what will likely be the results?

Digging Deeper:

1. How is a slingshot similar to a catapult? What are the differences? Who in the Bible effectively used a slingshot? Why was it effective in this war scenario?

2. Read Ezekiel 47:3-5 and compare it to what the author says in paragraphs three and four.

What are your thoughts about wading into the deep or catapulting into the deep?

3. In nature, what do you think could be compared to a catapult?

Worksheet

Catapult

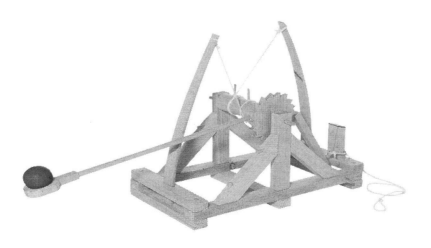

Chapter 26

Live While You Wait

Fill in the Blank:

1. We can all do something while we are waiting that is _____ in one way or another.

2. We should live our lives like Jesus is coming _____ or even today.

3. When we are productive, it usually motivates others to be _____.

4. We are doers, because we are about the _____ _____.

Discussion Questions:

1. Give some constructive ideas about things to do while waiting in a doctor's office or waiting in line at the grocery.

2. What story in the Bible illustrates waiting and what we should be doing? Give the Scripture reference.

3. How are Christians being productive while they wait for the second coming of Christ?

4. The last words of this chapter are "Choose well." What do you think the author meant by these words?

Group Activity:

Brainstorm activities to do while waiting with your children in a doctor's office. Are any of the activities constructive? Should activities always by constructive? Is there anything wrong with a child being entertained while waiting to see the doctor? Suggest some forms of quiet entertainment, as well as constructive, quiet activities.

Digging Deeper:

Go to the Internet and research the ancient Jewish customs of betrothal and marriage.

How do these symbolize the coming "Marriage Supper of the Lamb"?

Chapter 27

Oh Ye of Superpower

Fill in the Blank:

1. God is the supernatural, the _____.

2. _____makes us think more of ourselves than we should.

3. It benefits mankind when we see beyond our _____.

4. We cannot fully realize how _____ _____ to our brothers and sisters may change their lives.

Discussion Questions:

1. How does pride cause us to think more of ourselves than we should?

2. Is all pride bad? Explain.

3. What does it take to get rid of pride in our lives?

Group Activity:

Ask someone to read Luke 18:9-14. Discuss the role pride played in this parable. What was the outcome of the parable? Is pride observable in a church service today? How so? What lesson are we supposed to take away from this parable?

Digging Deeper:

• Find out what the Bible has to say about pride and the fall of Satan. What should that story tell us about pride?

• Find out what Solomon had to say about pride in the Book of Proverbs.

• Read Obadiah 1:3 and discuss the implications of pride in this verse.

- Ultimately, what should we do about pride in our lives?

Chapter 28

Peace: A Companion to Gratefulness

Fill in the Blank:

1. When we lose our _____, we tend to lose other things as well.

2. Engaging in conversation shows us when we are worried, because we can't seem to _____.

3. In the middle of a disquieted spirit, we are supposed to be _____.

4. As we lift up _____ in prayer . . . our load becomes _____.

Discussion Questions:

1. How does a believer lose peace?

2. What are the signs that we have lost our peace?

3. How do we get our peace back?

4. What does gratefulness have to do with peace?

Group Activity:

Brainstorm things that rob us of our peace.

Read the story about Jesus calming the wind and the storm on the Sea of Galilee (Mark 4). Compose a list of things we do to calm our fears. What should we do?

Digging Deeper:

Search the Scriptures about "gratefulness."

How does gratefulness bring peace?

Chapter 29

When Freshwater Meets Saltwater

Fill in the Blank:

1. God speaks to us _____.

2. The common factor between the natural and the spiritual is _____.

3. In the mixing of saltwater and freshwater, there is _____; because when they meet, a change has to take place.

4. When sin meets righteousness . . . a transformation takes place. Something _____ and _____ emerges.

Discussion Question:

1. The author draws a comparison of the confluence of saltwater and freshwater to the confluence of sin and righteousness. Discuss this occurrence in nature and in a spiritual sense.

2. How does the word "turbulence" influence the above comparisons?

3. The author says, "When the transformation takes place, something new and profound emerges." What is the "something"? Explain.

Group Activity:

If you have a science instructor in your group, ask him/her to explain how the estuary works. If you do not have a science instructor in your group, go to the *National Geographic* website on estuaries and read about the different kinds of estuaries (bay, lagoon, sound, and slough) and how they support an ecosystem.

Can sin and righteousness live together? Explain what happens when the two meet? Find some scriptures to support your answer.

Digging Deeper:

Look up the following scriptures about sin and righteousness: Romans 6:13, 18; 1 Corinthians 15:34.

Write down your own experience with sin and righteousness. How can you use this as a testimony when witnessing to others?

Chapter 30

You're Exhausted!
Or Have You Noticed?

Fill in the Blank:

1. We all prove inadequate in one way or the other in _____.

2. In relating the many activities her husband was involved in, the author says finally, "Oh, yes, and a _____ _____.

3. After diagnosis, the author says her husband "needed to realize there was a _____ _____."

4. At the hospital, a friend related a vision of a _____ set before [the author's husband] held by the _____ ____ _____.

Discussion Questions:

1. Explain what you think the author meant with her statement: "We all prove inadequate in one way or the other in communication."

2. Can you ever get too busy doing work for the Lord? Explain your answer and support it with scriptures.

3. What is your opinion of the vision related on p. 60?

Group Activity:

Research the side effects of burnout. Does burnout occur in only leaders and professionals? Check the Internet for statistics.

Come up with 10 destress activities or games.

Example: Take in a deep breath all the way to the top of your head and count 1-2-3; then exhale all the way to the tip of your toes and count 1-2-3. Then breathe normally.

Example: When you go home, take five to ten minutes to pet or play with your cat or dog.

Digging Deeper:

1. Read the story of Moses leading Israel out of Egypt. His father-in-law watched him one day settling disputes. Jethro gave his son-in-law some great advice on burnout (Exodus 18).

2. Examine your own life. Are you experiencing stress or burnout? If so, what can you do about it?

Chapter 31

Are You Willing to Give It Up?

Fill in the Blank:

1. A life without sacrifice is a life without _____.

2. Have you noticed when you pray for _____, God gives you tons of things that require it?

3. Our _____ being in Christ will provide all that is essential while living a sacrificial life.

4. _____ follows sacrifice.

Discussion Questions:

1. In your opinion, what is the theme of this lesson?

2. What does a sacrificial life consist of?

3. What is the "it" in the title of this lesson?

4. How does choosing hope help us deal with a problem psychologically?

Group Activity:

On the next page, read the examples of those who sacrificed for others.

Did these individuals have hope? If so, what do you think they hoped for? Do people today sacrifice for the good of others? Can you name someone?

What is the advantage of sacrificing for others?

Consider the scripture verses on the next page. How can we as Christ-followers fulfill these verses?

Digging Deeper:

Read the story of a time when David sinned by numbering the people (2 Samuel 24:10-25). The author uses 2 Samuel 24:24 as one of the verses to conclude this lesson. The verse has to do with cost and sacrifice. Why do you think David said he could not offer burnt offerings with "that which costs me nothing"? How does this concept apply to us today?

Chapter 31
Worksheet

Are You Willing to Give It Up?

Examples of Those Who Sacrificed

William Tyndale (1494 – 1536). Tyndale translated the Bible into English, which at the time was forbidden. For his controversial views and belief that everyone should be able to read the Bible in their native tongue, he was later arrested and executed.

Mother Teresa (1910 – 1997). Born in Albania, Mother Teresa left for India with virtually no money and devoted her life to serving the poor of Calcutta—overcoming poverty, disease, and criticism. She expanded her mission to support the poor and disadvantaged across the world.

Nelson Mandela (1918 – 2013). Nelson Mandela had the courage to fight against the unjust system of apartheid. For his political activities, he was sentenced to 20 years in prison, but he was released to lead a free South Africa.

Martin Luther King (1929 – 1968). King was a symbol of the fight against racial discrimination. Martin Luther King passionately supported the Civil Rights Movement, despite virulent opposition and discrimination in parts of America.

Scriptures About Sacrifice

"Through Jesus, therefore, let us continually offer to God a sacrifice of praise—the fruit of lips that openly profess his name" (Hebrews 13:15 NIV).

"Therefore, I urge you, brothers and sisters, in view of God's mercy, to offer your bodies as a living sacrifice, holy and pleasing to God—this is your true and proper worship" (Romans 12:1 NIV).

"But do not forget to do good and to share, for with such sacrifices God is well pleased" (Hebrews 13:16 NKJV).

Chapter 32

Make an Exchange

Fill in the Blank:

1. Wouldn't it be a greater yield to be deliberate in considering a higher level of _____ ?

2. When it comes to overcoming spiritual hurdles, the _____ at church is one of the best ways.

3. Leave it at the altar and take God's _____ with you.

4. That's the exchange: _____ _____ _____ .

Discussion Questions:

1. Does God want us to have more than enough to just get by in our everyday lives? Can your answer be supported by Scripture?

2. What does God say about our spiritual lives? Does God give us an abundance of His grace and power, or just enough to get us by each day? Support your answer with scriptures.

3. Explain Isaiah 61:3.

Group Activity:

If your group has their laptops with them, look up swapping or exchanging online. Look at the many different sites. The author advises to trade up—get rid of old items and get something new. Is this possible with online swapping? How is it possible spiritually? Explain.

Digging Deeper:

1. Read Isaiah 58:6-9. What is God saying through Isaiah the prophet? Does this affect us today? What did Jesus say that is somewhat similar? Where is it found in the Bible?

2. Read Matthew 16:26. Answer Jesus' question in this verse.

85 | *Make an Exchange*

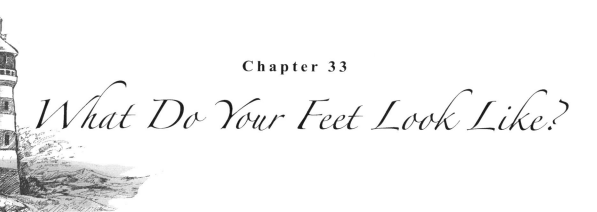

What Do Your Feet Look Like?

Fill in the Blank:

1. Our feet carry us _____ _____ _____ of mind-boggling journeys.

2. So, whatever your feet look like, try not to take them for _____.

3. God _____, _____, and _____ to use all His children who are willing.

4. All of us need to see beyond a _____ challenge.

Discussion Questions:

1. Should we care or not care about what our feet look like? Explain.

2. How does God use people who perhaps cannot stand on their feet or they have their mobility restricted? Give some examples of how they work for God.

3. Are handicapped people ineffectual because they have lost use of some part of their body? Explain.

4 Explain the analogy of the feet in Ephesians 6:15. (Example: What does being prepared with the gospel of peace have to do with feet?)

Group Activity:

Ask each member of the group to find a verse about "feet" in the Bible. Ask volunteers to read their verse and explain it. How does it have meaning for us today?

Digging Deeper:

Read Isaiah 52:7 and Romans 10:15. Paul in the Book of Romans is quoting from the passage in Isaiah. Explain this passage about "beautiful feet." Why are they called beautiful?

87 | *What Do Your Feet Look Like?*

In the New Testament, Jesus had his feet washed with tears (see Luke 7:44). In the Book of John is the story of Jesus washing the disciples' feet (see John 13:12-14). What is the symbolism of the feet being washed in both these stories? What, if anything, applies to us today?

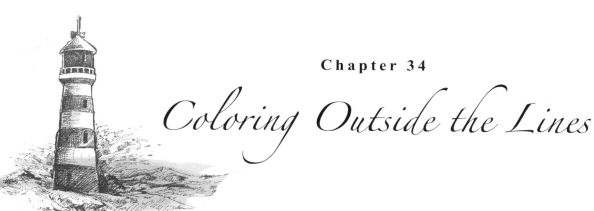

Chapter 34

Coloring Outside the Lines

Fill in the Blank:

1. People will, to varying degrees, attempt to keep within the lines or _____ as they mature.

2. Any good leader walks in a _____ open forum for suggestions and comments.

3. When we operate outside our realm of _____, the atmosphere is disturbed, because it conflicts with another's _____ and their assignment.

4. It is not man who ultimately promotes you; it is _____ your _____.

Discussion Questions:

1. What are the lines or boundaries to which the author refers in the second paragraph on page 67? Give examples.

2. If God were to give you the assignment of helping feed the poor, where do you think would be your "realm of authority"? Explain your thoughts.

3. What happens if, in carrying out your God-given assignment, you overstep your boundaries into someone else's territory? How would you go about working out the problem?

Group Activity and Digging Deeper:

Divide into groups of three or four. Each group will work on the following project:

Organize and implement a prayer ministry. Then, decide whether to conduct this prayer ministry in your local church or outside your local church. Next set a goal or goals for this prayer ministry. Who will be involved in this ministry? Will children be involved? If so, what ages and at what level will you involve them in the ministry? How many leaders and participants will you recruit? Do you need resources for this prayer ministry? If so, what kind? What will be the focus for this prayer ministry? Will your prayer ministry be "outside the box"? How? How many times will you meet and when?

Examples: Some have prayed for their city while walking around an area of focus. Others have met at a local school and prayed for God's protection over the students and faculty.

Hint: Your group may want to keep a journal of prayer times, where you prayed, and the focus of your prayer. Then, leave room for recording the answers to your prayers.

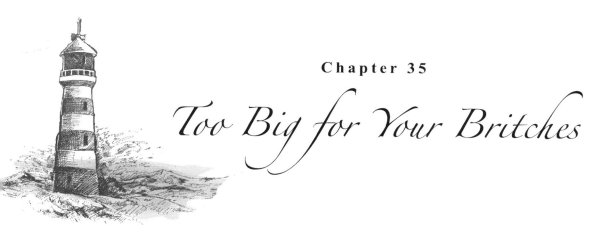

Chapter 35

Too Big for Your Britches

Fill in the Blank:

1. It is vital to seek_____ all the days of our lives with the same likeness as that of an accomplished student.

2. _____ is imparted by God, and it accompanies knowledge and understanding.

3. The more knowledge we acquire, definitely the more _____ we need.

4. Just because we know something doesn't make it wise to _____ it.

Discussion Questions:

1. Explain the title of this lesson.

2. What does the Bible say about acquiring wisdom? Give scripture references to support your answer.

3. What is the difference between *knowledge* and *wisdom*?

4. Explain what you think the author meant when she said: "Just because we know something doesn't make it wise to implement it." Give some examples.

Group Activity:

Divide into two groups. Ask one group to do a word study on the word *knowledge*. Ask the other group to do a word study on the word *wisdom*. Ask a member of each group to share their results. Now ask the group which is more necessary when trying to solve a legal problem, a household dispute, children's squabbles, a relationship problem, etc. What is their combined conclusion about acquiring these two items?

Digging Deeper:

1. From a spiritual standpoint, Solomon asked God for wisdom. Solomon makes a statement in Proverbs 1:7: "The fear of the Lord is the beginning of knowledge." Explain what this means.

2. Solomon addresses his son in Proverbs, chapters 2–7. What advice did Solomon give his son about acquiring wisdom?

Chapter 36

Tension

Fill in the Blanks:

1. When referring to a sewing machine, if the tension is set too loose, the stitches will not have a tight enough connection, and _____ _____ will result.

2. If the tension knob is set too tight, the _____ will get jumbled and the sewing needle cannot move_____.

3. There's another kind of tension that isn't related to a sewing machine, but it still involves holding something together. _____ comes because we don't know how we will be affected by any given situation.

4. Whatever comes up _____, we should deal with and not heap one thing on top of another.

Discussion Questions:

1. If humans had tension knobs like sewing machines, where would yours be set . . .

    a. When an argument is taking place among your children?

    b. When a romantic dinner is taking place between you and your spouse, or your special someone?

    c. When a heated discussion is taking place at work?

    d. Right now?

2. What do you think the author means by "heaping one thing on top of another"? Is it wise to do so?

3. Is it possible to adjust our tension when we are stressed? How?

Group Activity:

If you have your laptop with you, go to www.anxietycentre.com/stress-test/stress-test.shtml. This site has a free test you may take and get an instant score.

If you do not have your laptop with you, do the stress test at home and see your results.

Your score will give you an idea of where you stand as far as anxiety and tension in your life.

Digging Deeper:

Look up scriptures that deal with anxiety, burdens, etc.

Read 1 Corinthians 10:13.

Chapter 37

Trend Setters

Fill in the Blank:

1. Whether you wear fashionable clothing or not is less a concern than how you _____ _____ .

2. Any false desire leaves us _____ and _____ for more, because we are never satisfied.

3. Living within my means is an important _____ .

4. Let's pull in the reins of _____ .

Discussion Questions:

1. Why is it that people want to dress in the latest fashion? Is this considered a human flaw? Why or why not? What does the author say about this?

2. What does Jesus say about dressing in the latest fashion? (See Jesus Sermon on the Mount: Matthew 6:25-34.)

3. What does the author mean when she says, "Let's pull in the reins of comparison"?

4. Why is "living within our means" an important lifestyle? Explain.

Group Activity:

Go to the Internet and look up the latest trends among teens. List them and discuss their dangers. Why is it that teens are especially vulnerable to fashion and trends?

Discuss ways Christian teens can avoid falling into this habit of following trends.

Are adults also vulnerable to trends (keeping up with the trendy neighbors)? How can Christian adults stop comparing themselves to their peers? What should be a Christian's full focus?

Digging Deeper:

Who were the trendsetters in Jesus' day? What did Jesus have to say about them? Read the worksheet for Chapter 37 for additional information.

Read and consider the three scriptures which the author provides at the end of this lesson. What do they say to you?

Worksheet

Fashion, Faith and Following Jesus

By **Dan Blythe**

October 1, 2012

In the world of fashion or music, you get four types of people. You get the innovators, the trend-setters, the trend-followers, and then the mainstreamers.

It works like this:

The innovators will come up with some out-there idea. A raw sound or an outfit that will be reasonably radical and slightly weird. It won't be in fashion at that precise moment in time, but their idea is different, fresh, and oozes with potential.

The trendsetter is the person with influence. They are the ones who take it to the street, who wear it in the magazines, and get the thumbs up or thumbs down from the press. They are the risk-takers but not the creator; they didn't come up with the idea, concept, or sound.

The trend-follower is the one who takes what is good, what is popular, and then struts their stuff with their new attire. There is no risk here because they know what is in fashion. The shops have told them, the magazines have told them, and their celebrity role model has told them.

The mainstreamer is the person who follows the common current thought of the majority. In terms of music, it is the tunes in the top 20 that get pumped out on most radio stations. In clothes, it is the garments in the shop window of the most popular brands. There is nothing wrong with being mainstream. In fact, most people are. The mainstreamers keep the others in business.

So what does this have to do with anything I normally write about?

Fashion, music, and style will come and go. It is something that is always changing and morphing into something different. We can easily be maneuvered to look a certain way and to like a certain style. Sometimes, the directing is obvious, and other times, very hidden. Driven by the desire to fit in, we lose our individuality and personal innovation. Not everyone will design clothes or make music, but surely, we have a choice in who and what we follow?

Jesus is the same yesterday, today, and forever (Hebrews 13:8).

He does not fade away and does not come in or out of fashion.

From the moment He walked on Earth, He has been the most talked about person and even to this day remains in that position.

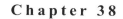

Chapter 38

There's Action Even If You're Still

Fill in the Blank:

1. My body says I'm still, yet my mind is _____.

2. God gave us a _____ mind.

3. If God authors something for you to do, He will enable you in _____, _____, and _____.

4. One of the most advantageous benefits you get from traveling in one place is allowing God to do the _____.

Discussion Questions:

1. Is daydreaming ever profitable?

2. The author says God gave us creative minds. What do you think God wants us to do with our creative minds? How do we know God's plans for our lives?

3. The author says, "Being in one place can be an extremely spiritual time." Is this true? If so, how is it spiritual?

4. Why do modern people feel like they have to be doing something all the time? (Otherwise, they feel like they are wasting time.) Is that your lifestyle—always moving, always doing something?

Group Activity:

Ask the group to sit silently without moving or talking for five minutes. (The facilitator should time this activity.) When the time is up, ask the group the following questions.

1. Was the time of not moving around difficult for you? Why?

2. What were you thinking about during the five minutes of silence?

3. Did you plan tomorrow's activities?

4. Did you use the time to pray?

As a group, what is your consensus about sitting still and silent? Is it profitable for you? Why?

Digging Deeper:

The author used Psalm 46:10 as one of her closing scriptures. Go to the Internet and research this scripture. Find out what the theologians say about its meaning. How do you feel now, after studying this lesson, about "sitting still"?

Chapter 39

Mirror, Mirror on the Wall

Fill in the Blanks:

1. We can't depend on fantasy to help us, so we depend on trusted ones in our lives to help us see _____, _____, and _____.

2. The testing element when hearing surprising or even shocking news about oneself is to ask the question: "Is there any _____ to what I've been told?"

3. God has used others, specifically family and close friends, as a _____.

4. Don't let _____ keep you from receiving _____ direction.

Discussion Questions:

1. If you had a "talking mirror" that always told you the truth, what question would you ask the mirror? Why?

2. Who in your life gives you honest answers and assessments? How do you respond to this information? Is this a good thing or a bad thing? Why?

3. The author says we should have a close friend hold us accountable. Do you agree with this advice? On what issues should we be held accountable?

4. The author uses Proverbs 16:18 at the end of this lesson. Explain how this verse ties in with the theme of the lesson.

Group Activity:

Look at the Worksheet of Emotional People on the next page. Consider the emotions you see.

If you were a mirror talking to each of these people, what would you say to them? What advice would you give them?

Digging Deeper:

Read the scriptures at the end of the chapter and consider them.

What do you think each of these scriptures is saying to you?

Chapter 39
Worksheet

Emotional People

Chapter 40

Emotions Run Amuck

Fill in the Blank:

1. It's up to me to discover how to experience my God-given_____.

2. Emotions can be _____ and _____, but they can break down spiritual walls between people.

3. A frantic state of mind is a mind without _____.

4. The Lord can make a _____ when there seems to be no _____.

Discussion Questions:

1. Define the word *emotion*. Name some of the eight basic human emotions listed by psychologists.

2. Which emotions can be dangerous? How are they dangerous?

3. Which emotions can be euphoric? What might cause euphoria or extreme happiness?

4. After an emotional upset and we calm down, where should we go for help? What is God's promise to believers?

Group Activity:

Ask the group to respond to the following case scenario:

> One day a lady in a brand new Volvo had been driving around a crowded parking lot and had finally found a spot. She was just about to back into it when a young man in a hotrod whizzed into the spot before her. As the young driver got out of his car and was walking away, the lady in the Volvo called out, "I found that spot first. What gives you the right to push in and take it?" The young man laughed and said, "Because I'm young and quick" and kept on walking.

What emotions would you experience if you were the lady in the Volvo? How would you react?

Digging Deeper:

Select three different emotions and look up scripture verses that deal with these particular emotions.

See attached worksheet for additional information.

What Are the Top Ten Human Emotions?

- **Fear** → Fear is an emotional response to a perceived external threat.

- **Anger** → Anger is feeling angry or experiencing rage.

- **Sadness** → Sadness is a feeling of loss, disappointment, or helplessness.

- **Joy** → Joy is a feeling of happiness and gladness.

- **Disgust** → Disgust is a feeling of something wrong, disgusting, or dirty.

- **Trust** → Trust is a positive emotion; admiration is stronger.

- **Anticipation** → Anticipation is a feeling of looking forward to an expected positive event or experience.

- **Surprise** → Surprise is how one feels when something unexpected happens.

- **Love** → Love is caring for someone. There are different kinds of love: Godly love, familial love, brotherly love, romantic love, etc.

- **Remorse** → Remorse is feelings of regret or shame.

Chapter 41

Are You on Solid Ground?

Fill in the Blank:

1. During an earthquake, you are never quite sure which way to run for_____.

2. Another thing about earthquakes is the inability to _____ for them.

3. It's important to realize that what goes on in the _____ eventually reaches the _____.

4. The Bible does give us _____ for remaining on the good path so our feet will not _____.

Discussion Questions:

1. Have you ever experienced an earthquake? How did you react?

2. If you have never experienced an earthquake, have you experienced another kind of natural disaster like a hurricane or a flood? Were you able to help others? If so, how?

3. Do you think natural disasters are punishment from God for the sins of the world? Explain your opinion.

4. Make a comparison of being on "shaky" ground to someone not serving God.

Group Activity:

Ask the group to find examples of earthquakes in the Bible.

Ask volunteers to share their findings and why they occurred or are going to occur.

Where can we find solid ground?

Digging Deeper:

Read Matthew 27:50-54. Why do you think this earthquake occurred at Jesus' death?

Read Matthew 28:2-4. Another earthquake occurred at Jesus' resurrection. Why do you think this earthquake occurred just a few days after the one at the time of Jesus' death?

Chapter 42

No Lurking Allowed

Fill in the Blanks:

1. Anything that lurks is probably not something we want to _____.

2. When God reveals what is _____, we can then stand face-to-face in strength of what is targeting us.

3. Eve, while in the Garden of Eden, was the _____ for hidden things.

4. If we don't have understanding and awareness, we are unable to address what needs to be _____.

Discussion Questions:

1. Define *lurking*. Have you ever experienced something or someone "lurking"? Tell about the occasion.

2. Perhaps the first occurrence of "lurking" was found in the Garden of Eden. Relate the occasion and explain why Eve succumbed to the situation.

3. How can we be prepared spiritually to overcome anything that "lurks" near us?

4. Read Psalm 10:3-11 about the wicked and how they "lurk." Does this happen today? If so, give an example.

Group Activity:

Ask the group: Does Satan "lurk" or does he reveal himself to us? Read 1 Peter 5:8 and discuss if the lion is lurking or "pouncing"? How does this relate to us? Does Satan confront us or sneak up on us? How can we be aware of him? Ask the group to give "real life" examples.

Digging Deeper:

Read Ephesians 6:13-17.

Chapter 43

There's an Elephant in the Room

Fill in the Blanks:

1. The more we try to hide it [elephant] . . . the more _____ it grows, and the more it _____ authority.

2. The best way to address the elephant is _____.

3. When small, it can enter more easily without being _____.

4. As Christians, we need to address sin when it's _____. We don't want to learn to _____ it.

Discussion Questions:

1. What does the author mean by an "elephant in the room"?

2. The author tells about a dream she had where a baby elephant got into her church. What does the dream mean? What are some possibilities of a sin that could be called a "baby elephant"? How does one go about getting the elephant out of the church? Explain.

3. Has an "elephant" ever wrecked a church? Give an example.

4. What were some of the "elephants" or sins that Paul said were in the church at Corinth? How did he suggest getting rid of them?

Group Activity:

Ask a volunteer to read Joshua 7 (the entire chapter). What was the "elephant" in this case? How did Joshua get rid of the sin? In your opinion, was this punishment too harsh? Why?

Digging Deeper:

In the Scriptures, find the solution for "hidden sins."

Chapter 44

Light's Destiny

Fill in the Blank:

1. Light doesn't have a certain _____ per se but travels until it reaches an _____.

2. God created a _____, _____, and heavenly sky without limits.

3. Natural _____ from starry skies doesn't have a destiny; it simply _____.

4. Spiritual _____ brings with it an extraordinary presence that draws others to it.

Discussion Questions:

1. Someone has said, "Darkness is the absence of light." Do you agree? Explain this concept.

2. Read Genesis 1:14-19. What was the purpose for the lights God created? Will they always serve this purpose?

3. Explain how Christ followers are symbols of light. Support your answer with a scripture.

Group Activity:

Ask the group to check the Internet or Bible Gateway for "prophecies concerning the sun, moon, and stars." Discuss what is prophesied about the end times and the sun, moon, and stars.

Are we seeing any signs in the heavens today?

Digging Deeper:

Read the three verses at the end of this lesson.

Read Psalm 148:3-5; 1 Corinthians 15:41.

Read Isaiah 13:6-13; Joel 2:10-11; Revelation 8:12.

Chapter 45

Cry of the Nation

Fill in the Blank:

1. The governments of nations are _____ in need of the populous crying out in prayer.

2. There is a _____ of individuals who know where their future lies.

3. Our nation was founded on the _____.

4. Wrap your mind around the _____ upon whom you can depend.

Discussion Questions:

1. Why should we pray for our government and the leaders?

2. What political similarities can be seen between the opening of the New Testament and the times in which we live? Give several examples.

3. Does your voice matter at the polls? How do you know whether it does or not?

4. Several scriptures throughout the Bible speak of a "remnant." Are believers today considered a remnant? Will God always have a remnant of believers? Support your answer with Scripture.

Group Activity:

Ask a volunteer to read aloud Romans 13:1-7. Discuss what this passage means. If God appoints governmental rulers to their respective places, why vote?

Someone made the statement, "History has shown that a people who are following God will have good leaders, whereas, a people who reject God will have ungodly leaders."

Could it be the reverse? Perhaps an ungodly leader would lead good people to commit abominations before God. What are your thoughts about this quote?

Digging Deeper:

Read 2 Chronicles 7:14

What might God say to our nation today?

Chapter 46

Love the Unlovely

Fill in the Blank:

1. Beauty lies in the _____ of the _____.

2. We must see more than _____ and look _____ than a first impression.

3. Jesus said, "Love one another and that is the greatest _____."

4. If we all had artistic abilities, it would be eye opening to see everyone's _____ _____.

Discussion Questions:

1. The title says, "Love the Unlovely." Who fits into the category of "unlovely"? Why?

2. John 15:17 says, "These things I command you, that you love one another." Does this mean everybody, or just those in the church? In your opinion, how well do churchgoers keep this command? How are you personally keeping this command?

3. The author says, "You can't judge a book by its cover. We must see more than appearance and look deeper than a first impression." Have you ever been put in a position of having to love someone in Jesus' name in spite of his/her appearance? Relate the story and how you responded? If you could change your response now, would you? Why?

Group Activity:

Ask someone to read aloud the story on the next page.

Discuss how you would have reacted had you been in the position of a parishioner, usher, or pastor?

Digging Deeper:

Read the three verses the author used at the end of this lesson.

What do you think 2 Corinthians 10:12 means?

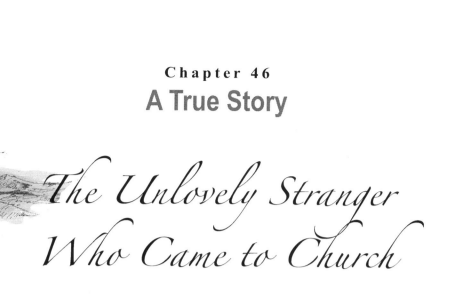

A True Story

The Unlovely Stranger Who Came to Church

A small group of faithful believers in a small community church were put to the test several years ago. The service had already started when the door opened to the sanctuary. A stranger walked in and found a seat near the front of the church. Everyone stared at the stranger because his appearance was less than desirable. He was dressed in dirty overalls, a plaid work shirt with stains, old shoes with no laces, and straw sticking out of his unkempt hair.

As the service progressed, people sitting behind the stranger began to quietly move to another part of the church; in fact, as far away from him as they could possibly get. It wasn't long until everybody in the church knew why. He smelled bad—actually bad is not the word. Perhaps unbearable would be a better word to use in this case. His clothes had not been washed—maybe never. It was summer, and the smell of sweat was very strong. However, that was not the worst of the smells—he was incontinent, so his clothes also smelled of urine.

The service soon closed—strangely enough, it seemed to be abbreviated. As soon as the "Amen" sounded, everyone exited the church as fast as they could. They needed fresh air. Everyone was asking who this stranger was; no one seemed to know where he came from. They had certainly never seen him in their community before. To tell the truth, they hoped they would never see him again.

Inside the church were the pastor, his family, and the stranger. The pastor, being a compassionate man, went to the stranger and introduced himself. He didn't just shake his hand, but he also hugged the stranger's neck. The pastor asked if he could help him in anyway. The stranger then briefly told the kind pastor that he was homeless and sick. The pastor offered to take him to a motel and pay for a room for the night. This offer was graciously accepted. The pastor also bought him some food and prayed with him.

The stranger returned to church several times, always with smelly clothes. He refused anymore offers of money or food. However, after one of the services, he accepted Christ as his Savior. Not long afterward, a small article in the newspaper told the stranger's demise.

He had no identification; no way of finding relatives; and the state buried him in a cheap coffin. He died of kidney failure. Appearances really did not matter to God, because God sees the heart.

—Nellie (Freeman) Keasling

Chapter 47

Feeling Lost?

Fill in the Blank:

1. If we could foresee the future, we wouldn't have to wonder about _____; but we would miss so much of the _____.

2. Our spiritual walk can be similar, because God wants us to _____ life to the fullest, not simply think about it.

3. The thrill of the journey is always going to be _____.

4. With God's help, don't be _____ of the unknown; be _____ for it.

Discussion Questions:

1. Have you ever been lost? What did you do about your situation?

2. The author says, "The thrill of the journey is always going to be risky." What do you think she meant?

3. In Luke 15, Jesus relates a parable of the shepherd who finds one lost sheep and is rejoicing. Why does he rejoice when he had 99 other sheep that were safe in the fold?

Group Activity:

Ask the group to participate in drawing a comparison of an individual's spiritual life to being lost and then found.

Imagine you and one other person are lost in a cave. Will you try to find your way out? What will no doubt happen? You may possibly have to stay in one spot until you are found. What will you eat and drink? Will you have any light?

Compare this experience to someone who is lost spiritually. How does he get found? Who finds and rescues him?

Digging Deeper:

Read Psalm 119:176; Luke 15:8-9; Luke 15:24; Luke 19:10.

Shackled in Chains

Fill in the Blank:

1. With shackles and chains, you have no _____ of how to get beyond a certain point.

2. Many people in the world today are _____ because they are _____.

3. The God of the universe can _____ chains that bind you.

4. With sincere hearts, we should desire for our children to accomplish more than we have, and it begins with a _____ _____.

Discussion Questions:

1. Read Acts 12:5-11. Peter describes being in jail and chained. How did he get out of prison? Why do you think Peter was spared being put to death at this time, but James (John's brother) was killed?

2. Are God's people today being imprisoned and perhaps shackled for the cause of Christ? If so, where? Who are the present-day martyrs for Christ?

3. What are some of the invisible chains that bind people today? How do they get loose from these chains?

Group Activity:

The author writes, "With sincere hearts, we should desire for our children to accomplish more than we have, and it begins with a pure heart." Find out what the Bible says about a "pure heart." Look up on the Internet, a Bible Concordance, or Bible Gateway, the phrase "pure heart." Describe how one goes from an "impure heart" to a "clean heart." Is this process something you are passing to your children? How are you doing this?

Digging Deeper:

Read the lyrics to "He Touched Me" by Bill and Gloria Gaither. They begin the song by referring to shackles and heavy burdens. What are the writers referring to? How do they get loose from the shackles? Can this be supported by scriptures in the Bible?

Chapter 49

A Wall for This and a Wall for That

Fill in the Blank:

1. Think of walls as assigning _____.

2. When the Israelites left Egypt, the Lord built a wall of _____ to protect them.

3. The people of Israel marched around _____ for seven days, and the walls came crashing down.

4. At times, we are _____ to tear down a wall; or we may opt to _____ ___ to what we have.

Discussion Questions:

1. Name some purposes for walls.

2. Are all walls desirable? Explain.

3. What are spiritual walls? Are they desirable? Explain your answer.

4. Ecclesiastes 3:3b says, ". . . a time to break down, and a time to build up." What is being broken down and what is being built up?

Group Activity:

In Robert Frost's poem "Mending Wall," the statement arises, "Good fences make good neighbors." Is this statement true? Again in the poem, the question is asked: "What are we walling in or what are we walling out?" How does this apply to the spiritual life?

Frost also says, "Something there is that doesn't love a wall." What is that "something?"

Digging Deeper:

How do you feel about a wall?

Chapter 50

Copy Cats

Fill in the Blank:

1. _____ doesn't make us smart; it postpones our _____.

2. When we were children, we _____, _____, and thought like children.

3. _____ moves us onward down the road to carve out for ourselves the inevitable likelihood of becoming and acting like an _____.

4. God's design for you is to be _____ in your own right.

Discussion Questions:

1. What childhood games did you play where you copied what your friends did? Did this game have a pleasing outcome? Why or why not?

2. When children enter their school years, especially secondary school, what happens if the need for copying continues?

3. Does the need to copy others continue into adulthood? Explain. Give an example of copying (or cheating) in adulthood.

4. What is God's design for our lives?

Group Activity and Digging Deeper:

Ask the group to divide into groups of three or four. Read the case study below on cheating. After a discussion among the members of your group, decide what should be done in the case.

> Jim is a senior and has only three more classes this semester before he graduates. He feels the pressure to maintain his 3.65 GPA, as well as just wanting to finish and get these classes out of the way.
>
> In one of his classes, an extra-credit assignment is to read through a set of given texts from certain articles and books that have been given by his instructor throughout the semester, and then to compile personal thoughts based on the principles covered. To Jim, it seemed

like doing something over he had already done in this class—read the same information again. He figured the instructor just wanted to make sure the students really did read the articles, so Jim wrote his paper using direct quotes and verbatim phrases from the reading without correct citation. It was just extra credit, after all, so if it turned out not to be as good as his other work, it didn't really matter or hurt his grade.

What do you predict will happen to Jim later as he goes into the workplace? Will this type of attitude ("it really didn't matter in this instance") carry over into his career? If so, what are the possible consequences? Does the Bible have anything to say about cheating?

Share your answers with the other groups in the group.

Chapter 51

Ask the Right Question

Fill in the Blank:

1. The Word will never lie to you, lead you _____, or _____ you.

2. The Word will forever teach, _____, enlighten, and be your _____.

3. Taking "me" out of the equation makes for a direct _____ to God's best.

4. Asking God a _____ is different from getting someone's _____.

Discussion Questions:

1. Jesus said in Matthew 7:7, "Ask, and it will be given to you; seek, and you will find; knock, and it will be opened to you." Does this mean we can ask for anything we want? Explain what you think this scripture means.

2. How important is motive when we ask things of God? Explain.

3. The author says, "Taking *me* out of the equation makes for a direct pathway to God's best." What does she mean? If you are asking something of God, how do you take "me" out of the equation?

4. How do you know when you are asking the "right question"?

Group Activity:

Ask the group to think of a time or situation in their lives when they did not know which way to turn for a solution to their problem. (Some possible situations might be career path, a turbulent relationship, a dream, finances, etc.) Now, ask them to write a letter to God explaining what they are troubled about. Close the letter by asking God the "right" question about how they should go forward from here. Many times, writing about the situation helps the person to think in an organized fashion and actually think a little more clearly about what they are asking. Then, ask the group to go home and pray about their situation.

Digging Deeper:

Consider the two questions in the story of the Good Samaritan (Luke 10:25-37).

Consider the questions Jesus asked in Luke 12:56-57.

Chapter 52

In Retrospect

Fill in the Blank:

1. Our future is a _____ of our _____.

2. We must learn from _____ and not _____ them.

3. Finish each season well, because that's how you will _____ the next.

4. When we endure and live to tell the tale, it's the very thing that hopefully _____ others from going through the same _____ and misery.

Discussion Questions:

1. Define retrospect.

2. The author says, "How can we tell if we are getting something right if we don't get a few things wrong?" Do you agree with her statement? Explain.

3. Is it true in your own life that you have made mistakes and learned from them? Give an example.

4. Do we gain knowledge or wisdom from our mistakes? Explain the difference.

Group Activity and Digging Deeper:

Ask one of the students to read the following case study:

> Ron, a businessman, was in a terrific hurry to leave home and get to his office for a meeting. He grabbed his dress jacket, his car keys, and his laptop case, and ran to get into his van in the driveway. As he approached his van, his laptop case suddenly opened up and his laptop crashed to the pavement. Horrified, he suddenly remembered he had not taken time to zip the case closed. He retrieved the laptop and hurried away to his meeting. In the back of his mind, he wondered if the laptop would still work. But, he did not take the time to check it until he arrived back home in the evening. When he did check it, it was indeed broken. Now, what would he do for a computer at work? He felt so dumb.

Discuss the following questions:

1. What mistakes did Ron make?

2. Considering the scenario, what will he need to do about getting another laptop?

3. If everyone makes mistakes, how should Ron feel about his mistakes?

4. What are the lessons to be learned?

5. How may Romans 15:4 help Ron?

Chapter 53

A Mother's Love

Fill in the Blank:

1. When He (God) awakens me in the middle of my nightly slumber and beckons me to get up and pray, I do so with _____ because there is a sense of _____.

2. God's Word says about love—it's the greatest _____.

3. Mothers stir and fan the flame of _____, igniting it to spread like _____.

4. When love is the _____, we more easily and quickly find _____.

Discussion Questions:

1. Is there a difference in a mother's love and a father's love when it comes to praying for their children? Explain.

2. Give Scripture verses about the "greatness" of love.

3. Explain the following line from this chapter: "When love is the catalyst, we more easily and quickly find truth." How is this true?

4. Share an example of your mother's love (or someone special to you).

Group Activity and Digging Deeper:

Ask someone in the group to read the enclosed story, titled "A Mother's Love." This is an analogy of the circle of life from the point of view of a mother's life, starting with motherhood.

Discuss the following questions about the story:

1. What was the catalyst in this story from the beginning to the end?

2. Why could the children say in the end, "You will always walk with us"? Is this statement and scenario true for every child?

3. Name some Bible women who fulfilled this loving role in motherhood.

4. If you have such a loving mother, have you shown your appreciation to her? Explain.

5. If our mothers have not fulfilled a loving role, do we honor them anyway? Why?

A Mother's Love

"Is this the long way?" asked the young mother as she set her foot on the path of life. And the Guide said:

"Yes, and the way is hard, and you will be old before you reach the end of it. But the end will be better than the beginning."

The young mother was happy, and she would not believe that anything could be better than these years. So she played with her children, she fed them and bathed them, taught them how to tie their shoes and ride a bike, and reminded them to feed the dog and do their homework and brush their teeth. The sun shone on them and the young mother cried,

"Nothing will ever be lovelier than this."

Then the nights came, and the storms, and the path was sometimes dark, and the children shook with fear and cold, but the mother drew them close and covered them with her arms. The children said,

"Mother, we are not afraid, for you are near, and no harm can come."

And the morning came, and there was a hill ahead, and the children climbed and grew weary, and the mother was weary. But at all times she said to the children,

"A little patience and we are there."

So the children climbed, and as they climbed they learned to weather the storms. And with this, she gave them strength to face the world. Year after year she showed them compassion, understanding, hope, but most of all unconditional love. And when they reached the top they said,

"Mother, we could not have done it without you."

The days went on, and the weeks and the months and the years. The mother grew old and she became little and bent. But her children were tall and strong, and walked with courage. And the mother, when she lay down at night, looked up at the stars and said:

"This is a better day than the last, for my children have learned so much and
are now passing these traits on to their children."

And when the way became rough for her, they lifted her, and gave her strength, just as she had given them hers. One day they came to a hill, and beyond the hill they could see a shining road and golden gates flung wide. And Mother said,

"I have reached the end of my journey. And now I know the end is better than the beginning, for my children can walk with dignity and pride, with their heads held high, and so can their children after them."

And the children said,

"You will always walk with us, Mother, even when you have gone through the gates."

And they stood and watched her as she went on alone, and the gates closed after her. And they said,

"We cannot see her, but she is with us still."

A mother is more than a memory. She is a living presence. Your Mother is always with you. She's the whisper of the leaves as you walk down the street, she's the smell of certain foods you remember, flowers you pick and perfume that she wore, she's the cool hand on your brow when you're not feeling well, she's your breath in the air on a cold winter's day.

She is the sound of the rain that lulls you to sleep, the colors of a rainbow, she is your birthday morning. Your Mother lives inside your laughter. And she's crystallized in every teardrop.

A mother shows through in every emotion—happiness, sadness, fear, jealousy, love, hate, anger, helplessness, excitement, joy, sorrow—and all the while hoping and praying you will only know the good feelings in life.

She's the place you came from, your first home, and she's the map you follow with every step you take. She's your first love, your first friend, but nothing on earth can separate you—not time, not space, not even death!

Why is the loneliness of old people a problem in today's world? Who could forget their own mother in an institution or old people's home and never visit them? Sure there are moments our mothers can get to our nerves—but just remember how many times it was the other way around.

Does not your mother's love, years of it, make her worthy of your attention? A mother's love is something you will always miss once she is gone. Even though she may not always know how to show it in a way we would understand, just remember that behind her calls, her worry, her suggestions for your life is love, and the wish you would do well in your life.

So show respect for your mother's love—a mother's love for her children never dies. Remember her, call her, visit her, ask her over to visit. One day you will be glad you did.

This is one of the most beautiful stories about a mother's love. It was written for *Good Housekeeping* magazine in 1933 by Temple Bailey. This is a story we should all read once in a while so we remember to respect our mothers for their love and guidance.

—Taken from the Internet

Chapter 54

Selective Blindness

Fill in the Blank:

1. He (God) shields our _____ and closes our ears at certain times to _____ us.

2. Part of our not seeing and hearing is because we are in _____.

3. We must give it a try to _____ _____ as best we can.

4. Resigning yourself to recognize the _____ of _____ is always in your best interest.

Discussion Questions:

1. What is "selective blindness"? Give an example.

2. According to the author, sometimes God reveals the plans for our lives one step at a time. Why do you think that is?

3. The author says, "Part of our not seeing and hearing is because we are in preparation." What is the *preparation* the author is referring to? Explain.

4. The last line of the devotion says, "Resigning yourself to recognize the voice of God is always in your best interest." Explain why this statement is true.

Group Activity and Digging Deeper:

Divide into groups of three or four. Ask them to read the following and answer the questions. Perhaps someone from each group could share their answers.

Predicting our life span is big business, government insurance and pensions spend billions of dollars predicting our death. A life table gives such an estimate. And the spooky part is that some statisticians think they can predict the time of our death within a three-year margin of error when provided with certain information. But death is not the great equalizer; gender and race have a huge effect on when the grim reaper will likely knock at your door.

1. If you could predict the future, would you want to know the exact date of your death? Why or why not?

2. The author asks the question: "Do we really believe something goes away if we ignore it?" How do you answer this question?

3. Some people ignore the fact that one day they will die and stand before God in judgment. How should Christians deal with this kind of individual?

4. Do some people (even believers) have "selective blindness" when it comes to spiritual things? Give examples.

5. Can you find scriptural examples of "selective blindness"?

Chapter 55

Rise and Shine

Fill in the Blank:

1. As believers, we are able to see the splendid _____ of creation every day with _____.

2. No matter what our _____ or what kind of morning person we are, God is _____ and wants to spend the day with us.

3. Whatever God allowed in my _____ was preparation for something _____.

4. Start your day with the _____ _____, and you will notice how much He loves spending time with you.

Discussion Questions:

1. The author uses a figure of speech (simile) in the first paragraph: "Just like we can't see to drive well and safely in foggy weather, neither can we see well to make good decisions when our minds aren't clear." Can you take this comparison a step further and make a spiritual comparison?

2. Do you carry over problems from the previous day into your new day? If so, how to you resolve them? If you don't want to carry over problems, how do you go about resolving them before bedtime?

3. The author writes: "Whatever God allowed in my yesterday was preparation for something today." Explain this statement.

4. How do you recognize when God is helping you solve a problem? Explain.

Group Activity:

Divide your group into two groups: (1) Those who enjoy mornings and have no trouble getting up, and (2) Those who hate the alarm clock and never want to get up. Ask each group to come up with a list of 10 things to get their mornings started for success. Finally, ask each group to present their list to the group.

Digging Deeper:

Look up three scriptures that talk about "tomorrow" and how we should face it.

Chapter 56

Return to Innocence

Fill in the Blank:

1. Life is similar to a _____; upon entering, we must find a way _____.

2. No one has to recover from _____ decisions, so we want that which we do to be of _____.

3. Fortunately, we serve a _____heavenly Father who sees us with uttermost _____ affection and concern.

4. God is in the business of helping us get something _____, no matter how many times we get it _____.

Discussion Question:

1. Is there a way to achieve innocence? Explain.

2. Explain how life is similar to a maze.

3. How does our heavenly Father view us?

4. In the last sentence of this lesson, the author says that the Lord gives us back our innocence, but with experience that is "wisdom enriched." What do you think she meant by "wisdom enriched"? Explain.

Group Activity and Digging Deeper:

Ask the group to do an individual assignment. The author makes the statement that life is similar to a maze—we begin our lives at one end and continue through until we exit at the other end. Life happens in between the two.

Example: The individual might draw a road or timeline with important stops along the way (Birth [innocence] to childhood; teen years to young adulthood; adulthood to present). Where along the way did you lose your innocent state and where did you regain it through salvation? Where are you now in your journey?

Chapter 57

Between Hearts

Fill in the Blank:

1. The distance between hearts, relationally speaking, _____ any land or water mass.

2. It helps to be _____ in ways to close the gaps, before they become huge fissures; otherwise, it's impossible to _____ like we used to.

3. There isn't anything more valuable on earth than _____.

4. When we find ourselves distanced from God, we must bear in mind it isn't _____ who moved away.

Discussion Questions:

1. The author writes about her experience of moving away from friends and family, using the phrase, "we are 'weathered friends.'" Explain what you think she means.

2. The author explains it takes effort to keep in contact with distant friends. She asks the question: "Is the relationship worth the effort?" How do you personally answer that question? Why?

3. In the author's opinion, "There isn't anything more valuable on earth than relationship." Do you agree? Why or why not?

4. Have you experienced the pain of moving away from loved ones or dear friends? How did you deal with the situation? Looking back, would you do things differently today? How?

Group Activity and Digging Deeper:

Divide your group into pairs. Ask them to respond to the questions below.

1. Tell me your favorite ice cream flavor.

2. Tell me a wonderfully random childhood anecdote.

3. Recite your favorite Bible verse and tell why it is your favorite.

4. Have you ever needed someone to pray for/with you? What was the occasion? How did knowing someone was praying help you to deal with your problem?

These questions (and others) help you get to know another person better and build a relationship with him/her. What do you now know about this person that you did not know before? Will this knowledge help you to become closer spiritually? Why?

Now, answer the question: "How important are relationships?"

Chapter 58

Who Tracked in That Mud?

Fill in the Blank:

1. When someone points out our mistakes, and we are not _____, that is a good sign of _____.

2. If we justify our incorrect _____, we won't like it much when we see them responding to us in the same way.

3. A _____ person is more teachable and _____.

4. Be a person who learns from _____, no matter the individual whom God sends to teach us.

Discussion Questions:

1. How do you respond to your mistakes?

2. What is the appropriate attitude to making mistakes?

3. What is/are the consequence(s) of justifying your mistakes?

4. What response does God want or expect from us when we make mistakes? What scripture(s) will support your answer?

Group Activity:

Ask for two or three volunteers to relate a personal experience of making a mistake in life. What were the consequences? If this or something similar happened to you again, how would you handle it? What lessons have you learned?

Digging Deeper:

Read the following scriptures and think how you would react to the situation:

1. Read Matthew 26:69-75.

2. Read Matthew 27:1-5.

Chapter 59

The Battle Is His; the Choices Are Ours

Fill in the Blank:

1. Best choices are not always the _____, and many times we are _____ by distractions which come at us like darts from every direction.

2. _____ through trials can be very heated until things come to the surface.

3. Everything happens for some _____, and there is a _____ for all things.

4. God's plan for us is constantly in_____, and He is involved in all _____ of all matters.

Discussion Questions:

1. According to the author, what is the simple formula for a victorious outcome of the battle?

2. Who are our allies in the "race of life"?

3. What does the author say is our course of action?

4. Do you agree with the author's statement: "Everything happens for some reason, and there is a season for all things"?

Group Activity and Digging Deeper:

The Refiner's Fire

As she watched the silversmith, he held a piece of silver over the fire and let it heat up. He explained that in refining silver, one needed to hold the silver in the middle of the fire where the flames were hottest so as to burn away all the impurities. The woman thought about God holding us in such a hot spot; then she thought again about the verse that says: 'He sits as a refiner and purifier of silver' (Malachi 3:3). She asked the silversmith if it was true that he had to sit there in front of the fire the whole time the silver was being refined. The man answered that yes, he not only had to sit there holding the silver, but he had to keep his eyes on the silver the entire time it was in the fire. If the silver was left a moment too long in the flames, it would be destroyed. The woman was silent for a moment. Then she asked the silversmith, 'How do you know when the silver is fully refined?' He smiled at her and answered, 'Oh, that's easy — when I see my image in it.'

—Taken from the Internet
https://ourgoodwinjourney.com

Ask the group to make the comparison to our spiritual lives.

Chapter 60

Good Morning, Lord, It's Me

Fill in the Blank:

1. When I greet my Maker each morning, I am spiritually _____.

2. The Enemy desires to _____ the property of God—His _____.

3. Let's speak powerful _____ words out of our mouth as we encounter our _____ of the day.

4. I have made an inconsiderate remark because I wasn't feeling up to par; it set the day on a _____ _____.

Discussion Questions:

1. In your opinion, is it important to pray in the morning? Why?

2. If mornings are difficult or extremely busy, what can be an alternative for meeting early with the Almighty?

3. If you get too busy in the mornings to pray, how does your day go? Explain.

Group Activity:

Ask for volunteers to testify about their mornings with the Almighty.

Ask if anyone would be willing to testify about their evenings with the Almighty.

Should we do both? Why?

Digging Deeper:

1. Do a scripture search on the word "morning," especially when dealing with rising early and meeting with God.

2. Do a scripture search on the word "awake or awaken."

What do you think God is saying to His people about early morning time with Him?

Chapter 61

Do I Belong?

Fill in the Blank:

1. Being chosen for _____ is right up there with some of the best things that can happen to us.

2. The hardest and toughest of people have an innate sense to _____.

3. Throughout the word, there are countless _____ who want and need to be the recipient of a family _____.

4. There are _____ to overcome in most families, but there are none too big to _____.

Discussion Questions:

1. Why do you think the author wrote . . . "Being chosen for participation is right up there with some of the best things that can happen to us"? Explain your answer.

2. Why do adopted children understand the concept of being chosen more than children born naturally into a family?

3. How does "adoption" play into our spiritual experience with God?

4. Were you ever the child who was last to be chosen on a sports team? How did that experience make you feel? Will this ever happen to you spiritually? Why or why not?

Group Activity:

Divide into three or four groups and ask them to work on the following exercise:

Discuss and prioritize the following people or groups to which we belong: *Spouse, children, parents, church, school, God, friends, coworkers, neighbors, and cliques.*

Put these in order by most important to least important. Explain your order.

Digging Deeper:

Find at least three scriptures dealing with being God's "chosen" people.

Find three scriptures dealing with "adoption."

Chapter 62

Freshen Up

Fill in the Blank:

1. When you feel _____, there's nothing like a breath of _____ _____.

2. You can be used to bring _____ to others since you yourself are _____.

3. _____, more than likely, had to deal with the same _____ as we do today.

4. Making someone else more _____ than myself, is healing _____.

Discussion Questions:

1. What does the author recommend when the pressures of the day become overwhelming? Do you agree? Why?

2. Why would helping someone else "rejuvenate" you? Explain your thoughts on this.

3. The author writes: "We both shared a poignant moment mulling over the thought that nothingness could be a shroud over anyone." Explain this statement. Do you agree? Why?

4. What is wrong with a "pity party"? How do you get over a "pity party"?

Group Activity:

Divide into three groups. Ask each group to select one verse found at the end of the chapter. They will discuss among themselves what the verse means, and then someone from their group will present their findings to the class.

Digging Deeper:

Read the entirety of Psalms 42 and 43.

What are the differences? Is there a difference in Psalm 42:11 and Psalm 43:5? They ask the same question, but they come at the end of two different psalms. Do they show a different attitude? So, how does David refresh himself?

Chapter 63

Scared? Don't Be!

Fill in the Blank:

1. _____ to God will outweigh any _____ we have.

2. Each and every time _____ is in our face or whispers in our ear, we can choose to _____ it.

3. When we _____ fear, we find the gift of _____ awaiting us, as well as a sigh of relief.

4. Fear also comes in the form of _____.

Discussion Questions:

1. Where does fear come from?

2. How do we conquer our fears?

3. What are the differences in children's fears and adult fears?

4. What do you think the author means by the statement, "Fear also comes in the form of temptation"?

Group Activity:

Pass out small note cards—one per person—and ask each person to write their worst fear on the card. Then, pass a basket (or some receptacle) and collect the cards. Pass the basket again and ask each person to randomly select a card. Now, ask each person to read the fear written on the card and try to guess what has made that person become afraid of whatever is written on the card. For example, if you draw a card that says "the dark," perhaps the individual was afraid of the dark as a child and has never conquered it. After everyone has had a chance to read his/her card and comment, ask the group to suggest ways to overcome fear.

Digging Deeper:

Find three or more verses in the Bible that address the subject of overcoming fear.

Write them down and use them as reminders when you are afraid of a situation.

Who Did Jesus Run With?

Fill in the Blank:

1. As Christians, we stumble, fall, and roll along, making our way night and day right beside others of the _____ _____.

2. Jesus did run with _____ ones.

3. Reading about the _____ who walked with Christ teaches me a great deal about who _____ was, is, and always will be.

4. Instead of watching a _____ and withering away of brothers and sisters, enlist your servitude as _____ and _____ of a loving God.

Discussion Questions:

1. According to the author, Jesus had friends who were wayward and disreputable. Why?

2. Why would Jesus want to train men to preach the gospel who were uneducated, disreputable men? Could Jesus actually trust these men? Explain your answer.

3. Name some of the men Jesus chose to train and what they did in life. How did they turn out after Jesus went back to heaven? What made the difference?

4. Who do we run with today?

Individual Activity:

Ask the group to write their salvation testimony, including their previous life, salvation experience, and life since salvation. How different is their life today from their previous life as a sinner? Who do they run with today and why?

Digging Deeper:

Read the following verses and contemplate what they say to you:

Matthew 10:38; 16:24; 19:21.

159 | *Who Did Jesus Run With?*

Chapter 65

The Road That Leads Home

Fill in the Blank:

1. When my _____ _____ have been gone for a while, I have one thing in mind—flinging the _____ _____ wide open to greet them.

2. If it's not a _____ door, it's the door of the _____.

3. How can I call someone "_____ _____" if I'm not willing to show them _____?

4. Our children must find their spiritual _____ for themselves.

Discussion Questions:

1. The title of this lesson is "The Road That Leads Home." What road is she referring to? What "home" is she referring to?

2. Is there a spiritual analogy in this lesson? If so, explain it.

3. The author says, "Our children must find their spiritual path for themselves." How does that statement line up with the verse in Proverbs 22:6, which says, "Train up a child in the way he should go, and when he is old he will not depart from it"?

Group Activity:

Ask someone to read the story of the prodigal son found in Luke 15:11-32. Discuss the prodigal son's relationship with his father. Why do you think the prodigal son wanted to leave home? How does he come to his senses? How does Proverbs 22:6 line up with this story? Is it true for prodigals today? Will they always come home? Discuss the spiritual comparison of this story.

Digging Deeper:

Think about your life from birth to the present. Did your parents give you training in the early years and put you on the right road to eternity? If so, were there any detours? Write down your testimony and be prepared to share it with someone when there is opportunity.

If you did not have a Christian upbringing, how did you get on the right road to where you are today? Write down your testimony and be prepared to use it when there is opportunity.

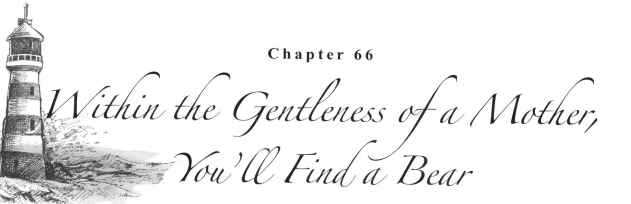

Chapter 66

Within the Gentleness of a Mother, You'll Find a Bear

Fill in the Blank:

1. _____takes a back seat to _____, as it should.

2. When I'm able to do something far greater than what my own natural abilities are, I'm experiencing what _____is doing.

3. If you _____the situation too long, you may fail to follow through with a _____action.

4. The ones who tap into what the Lord wants to do through them allow greater _____to occur.

Discussion Questions:

1. Explain the figure of speech in the title—a "bear."

2. The author says "fear" takes a back seat to "strength." When and how does this happen?

3. Give an example from the Bible where strength took over a seemingly helpless situation.

Group Activity:

Using the "bear" motif in the title, trace the comparison of strength throughout the devotional, including the personal illustration the author gives at the end of the devotional. Allow time for others in the group to give a personal illustration of supernatural strength in a catastrophic situation.

Digging Deeper:

The author uses three scriptures about strength at the end of the devotional. Find three more and write them down.

Chapter 67

Thank You, Ma'am— You're Welcome, Sir

Fill in the Blank:

1. _____ seems to have gone by the _____ in our simple everyday activities.

2. Our _____ can't seem to be obtained quickly enough.

3. It is important to not use an _____ for an _____.

4. It can't always be the _____ _____ that's the problem.

Discussion Questions:

1. Does the world of technology take the place of teaching our children politeness and good manners? What is your opinion?

2. The author asks the question: "How do I respond when I encounter rudeness?" What is your answer to this question?

3. What do you think the author meant by her statement: "It's important to not use an apology as an excuse"?

4. Does the Golden Rule apply in all areas of society?

Group Activity and Digging Deeper:

Look up Matthew 7:12 and ask someone in the class to read it aloud. How would you respond to the following scenario?

Recently, a Starbucks store had a customer ask for the key to the men's room. However, the employee refused to give the customer the key because he had not purchased anything. It seems he was waiting for a friend. The employee called the police and an uproar ensued.

As a Christian bystander, what would you have done? Would you have taken the side of the employee or the customer? Or, would you have done nothing? Does the Golden Rule apply to this story? How?

Chapter 68

Precious Cargo

Fill in the Blank:

1. How do you think we should package or care for our _____ when we send them on their way?

2. We teach them a variety of age-appropriate _____ so they are prepared for all kinds of _____.

3. We are _____ like a breath of _____.

4. _____ your gifts so they can edify and be ready for _____.

Discussion Questions:

1. What is the "precious cargo" the author is referring to in the title?

2. How does the author carry through this motif in the devotion?

3. Explain the simile "We are fragile like a breath of wind." Does this relate to the "precious cargo"? How?

4. The first scripture at the end of the devotion says, "Teach them to your children." What are we teaching?

Group Activity:

The last sentence of this devotion says, "Pass on the treasures of God that are inside your children and to their children's children."

Discuss what the "treasures" are that are being passed on to future generations.

Find scriptures to support this concept.

Digging Deeper:

Find five scriptures in the Bible that refer to children and how we as parents are to treat them as they grow up.

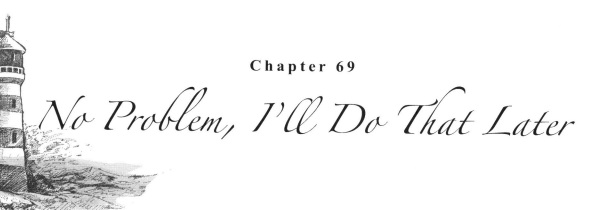

Chapter 69

No Problem, I'll Do That Later

Fill in the Blank:

1. The culprit is _____.

2. If we could only ask this question: "Is what I am about to _____, going to bring a _____ result in any way?"

3. _____ is a relative to _____.

4. If God _____ you to do something, He is _____ for showing you how to get it done.

Discussion Questions:

1. The author calls procrastination a "joy zapper." What does this mean?

2. The author says we can deceive ourselves by thinking we have plenty of time. How so? Give an example.

3. The author lists some phrases she has used regarding procrastination. Can you add three more to the list?

4. The author says, "Regret is a relative to procrastination." Explain how this is true.

Group Activity:

The author ends this devotion by saying, "If God authorizes you to do something, He is responsible for showing you how to get it done."

Ask the class for volunteers to share how God helped them to finish a task they felt led to do.

Digging Deeper:

Read the following scriptures on procrastination:

Proverbs 5:4; Proverbs 6:6-8; Proverbs 27:1.

Chapter 70

Drat Those Bad Habits!

Fill in the Blank:

1. You have to begin a new _____ habit to replace the old one.

2. Becoming overly focused on ending a _____ _____, we may fail to realize we're at a _____.

3. _____ review with sincere _____ is a way to keep things from sneaking up on us.

4. Those who _____ me most are the ones I'm counting on and who have earned the place in my life to speak _____ to me.

Discussion Questions:

1. How long does it take to stop a bad habit? Why do you think it takes this long?

2. The author says that stopping a bad habit is only half the task. Why is this true?

3. The author says sometimes bad habits can be unnoticed. How is that possible?

4. What is the solution to becoming aware of bad habits and getting rid of them?

Group Activity:

According to the author, it takes 30 days to stop a bad habit. Ask the class to research on the Internet how long it takes to form a good habit. How does one go about forming a good habit?

Give some examples of how to stop bad habits in adults for example, talking on the cell phone while at dinner with others. What good habit(s) replace the bad habit(s)?

Do Christians have bad habits? If so, how are they replaced? Give examples.

Digging Deeper:

Read the following scriptures: Proverbs 4 (entire chapter); Proverbs 9:10; 1 Corinthians 15:33.

Knock, Knock

Fill in the Blank:

1. _____ is a key factor when answering our front door these days.

2. How we wait upon the Lord for answers and direction will determine who _____

   _____.

3. _____ and _____ are two visitors who show up much too often without being invited.

4. _____ like one being _____gives us staying power necessary to ascertain God's leading.

Discussion Questions:

1. Discernment is a necessary quality we need to help protect ourselves in today's world. Speaking spiritually, explain how discernment helps us.

2. What keeps believers from allowing the guilt of the past to torment them?

3. How does the author use the "Knock, Knock" starter of her devotion to teach an important lesson on opening our spiritual "doors"? To whom should we open our heart's doors and to whom should we not open our doors? How do we know the difference?

Group Activity:

A lady who was saved from her sins later in life just cannot seem to forgive herself for past sins. She is troubled with remorse from time to time and often sits and weeps for days at a time. Someone told her she was allowing Satan to knock at her door, and she was listening to him condemn her for past sins.

Ask the group members to give this lady advice on how to forgive herself for past sins. What Scripture verses would help her?

Digging Deeper:

Find at least three Scripture verses that deal with discernment.

Chapter 72

The Butterfly

Fill in the Blank:

1. Unlike the butterfly, it is our _____ _____ that will outlast any _____ display of attractiveness we exhibit.

2. _____ is where lasting change takes place.

3. Before a _____ takes place, there has to be a season of _____.

4. When the Lord quiets you . . . He is beginning a _____ within you so that you will emerge _____.

Discussion Questions:

1. Describe the metamorphosis that occurs from a caterpillar to a butterfly.

2. Describe the similar change that occurs from a sinner to a saved individual.

3. Does a reverse metamorphosis ever occur in nature or in people? Explain.

4. When there are quiet times in our spiritual lives, does this mean God has abandoned us? Explain.

Group Activity:

Ask the group to define *metamorphosis*. (From the Greek, it means "a transforming.")

Ask the group to use their imagination and describe what a spiritual transformation of the heart would look like if we could watch it take place. (Hint: Some children's object lessons use dark food coloring to represent sin and then bleach to remove it. It is shown being demonstrated on YouTube: https://www.bing.com/videos/search?q=YouTube+on+forgiveness+using+food+coloring+and+bleach&&view=detail&mid=6F7DCAD54E87C790949D6F7DCAD54E87C790949D&rvsmid=2D9AE872C5C1925D66602D9AE-872C5C1925D6660&FORM=VDQVAP)

Digging Deeper:

How will our bodies be changed (transformed) into the likeness of Christ's resurrected body?

Chapter 73

Doubt Is Not Believable

Fill in the Blank:

1. Trading in _____ for _____ is definitely not trading up.

2. _____ closes the window of _____ and the hope that's available in all things.

3. Belief the size of a mustard seed of faith is _____.

4. We beat ourselves up with _____, a tool of the Enemy, instead of enriching our minds with _____.

Discussion Questions:

1. The author says, "I think we all experience a wedge of doubt that crosses the threshold of our minds and plans." As believers, how should this be handled? Find a Scripture reference to support your answer.

2. Why do you think believers doubt?

3. What is the definition of *faith*?

Group Activity and Digging Deeper:

Ask for someone to read Luke 1:5-22.

Zacharias was in the Temple when Gabriel—the angel who stands in God's presence—appeared to him and promised to give him and Elizabeth a son. He should have been ecstatic with joy. Every day for years this devout couple had prayed, "Lord, if it be Your will, give us a son." But that was years ago; now it was too late. They were both long past the time when couples were able to conceive. Zacharias had reconciled himself to reality—they were *not* going to have a son. He had come to terms with God over the matter. Perhaps, he said something like this: "God is sovereign. He is free to bestow His blessings on whomever He wishes. For some unknown reason, He withheld that blessing from us." And now, Zacharias was not willing to open himself to the roller coaster of hopes and fears that had long ago been left behind. And so he doubted the word of the angel.

What does Zacharias teach us about the problem of doubt?

Chapter 74

Me? Lazy?

Fill in the Blank:

1. I think most of us experience _____ days now and then.

2. Over the years, there has been evidence that some _____ would have benefitted my family and me.

3. We sharpen each other like _____ sharpens _____ because of His authority.

4. We can learn from each other without losing the _____ God created in each of us.

Discussion Questions:

1. Do you ever experience "lazy" days? What do you do on these kinds of days? Do you feel guilty? Why?

2. Do you use a calendar to schedule activities and appointments? Is this helpful? How?

3. Explain the phrase, "iron sharpens iron" as it relates to humans.

4. How do some people get so much done and others—in the same time frame—do not? What do you think their secret is? Should we all strive to be like the overachievers? Explain.

Group Activity and Digging Deeper:

Divide into three groups. Each group will take an assigned animal/insect and look up scriptures about their insect or animal. Then, go to the Internet and study the insect/animal and its ways. What can we learn from the animal/insect either positively or negatively about laziness?

Group 1: Ant

Group 2: Locust (Grasshopper in the locust family)

Group 3: Rock Badger (Rock Hyrax or "Dassie")

What are the spiritual lessons to be learned from the animal/insect that you were assigned?

Chapter 75

Does the Fire Really Need Another Log?

Fill in the Blank:

1. When it comes to disagreements, _____ can run _____.

2. Wrongdoings and _____ are shot like arrows of division, resulting in _____, anger, and _____.

3. Unearth a _____word first. Everyone needs _____, and it's an effective diffuser.

4. Respond in a way that is the _____ of . . . anger.

Discussion Questions:

1. The author makes a comparison of a disagreement being like a fire. Why is this a great comparison?

2. The author said she learned the method of responding in the opposite spirit. Explain what she means by "opposite spirit."

3. In your opinion, does this method work in solving a disagreement? Explain your answer.

4. Which beatitude goes with this lesson?

Group Activity and Digging Deeper:

As a group, read Matthew 5:3-10. Someone has suggested that the Beatitudes can be regarded as building blocks which rest one upon another—stepping stones that follow in succession. For example, the first one says, "Blessed are the poor in spirit, for theirs is the kingdom of heaven." This bankruptcy brings on mourning for sins and weaknesses. The next Beatitude says, "Blessed are those who mourn, for they shall be comforted." The comfort of the Holy Spirit brings a willingness to submit oneself completely to the Lord. Discuss how the other Beatitudes build upon each other until they come to being a "peacemaker."

Note: Dr. Mary Ruth Stone suggested the following summary concerning the Beatitudes:

Those who have recognized their poverty and who have mourned have entered the Kingdom and have become meek. They have received the righteousness, mercy, and purity of God and have seen His glory. Now and only now are they ready to be peacemakers.

Donald S. Aultman, ed. "Blessed Is the Peacemaker." *Leading With Integrity* (Cleveland, Tennessee: Pathway Press, 2004.

Chapter 76

Clandestine: My Secret Place

Fill in the Blank:

1. Wherever I am or whatever I am doing, [God] will _____ with me.

2. Many of us today miss the opportunity to spend _____ _____ with our "heavenly Planner."

3. Putting off things of vital _____ invites _____.

4. Seek _____ before you start your day.

Discussion Questions:

1. In Matthew 6:6, Jesus said, "When you pray, go into your closet" (KJV). What does the author call her prayer closet? What do you call yours?

2. What is the difference in "praying without ceasing" (1 Thessalonians 5:17 KJV) and praying in your "closet" at a specified time (mornings or evenings)? Can one do both? Explain.

3. Why is it important to get alone with God in a "secret place"? Give at least three reasons.

4. What are the ways you pray at church? Why are these types of prayers different from the ones you pray when alone with God?

Group Activity:

Ask the group to pray in response to the letters in the word PRAY.

P   **Praise**   Ask someone to lead in a few praise choruses which direct the minds and hearts to God.

R   **Repent**   Ask someone else to lead in a prayer of repentance (for sins of omission as well as commission).

A   **Ask**   Allow those who have a prayer request [and wouldn't mind saying it aloud] to submit a request for everyone to pray over as a group.

Y   **Your . . . own needs.** Close the meeting with everyone praying for his or her own needs.

Digging Deeper:

Since we are followers of Christ, we should pattern our prayer life after His. Using Bible Gateway on the Internet or a Bible Concordance, look up the times when Jesus prayed alone in a "secret" place.

Chapter 77

Masterpiece

Fill in the Blank:

1. How we treat someone should be a _____ of how we want to be treated.

2. We are all masterpieces and should be handled with _____care—care that causes us to _____.

3. All of us can call upon the ultimate Artist, the _____himself, who formed us and transforms us.

4. We were fashioned an _____ by the Potter himself.

Discussion Questions:

1. The author writes that we are all masterpieces and "should be handled with essential care." What do you think she means by "essential care"?

2. What, in your opinion, qualifies as a "masterpiece"?

3. In the third paragraph, the author uses a metaphor of an "artifact in disrepair." Trace this metaphor through the rest of the devotion. How do we compare to the metaphor?

Group Activity and Digging Deeper:

Ask someone to read aloud the attached story, "The Son."

Ask the following questions:

1. Why does the painting of the son become a masterpiece for the father?

2. How does this compare to God and His Son?

3. The gardener who bought the painting of the son suddenly became a wealthy man. How does the gardener compare to mankind, with one exception?

4. The auctioneer's closing words—"whoever takes the Son, gets everything"—teaches us what message?

185 | *Masterpiece*

Chapter 77
Story

The Son

A wealthy man and his son loved to collect rare works of art. They had everything in their collection, from Picasso to Raphael. They would often sit together and admire the great works of art. When the Vietnam conflict broke out, the son went to war.

He was very courageous and died in battle while rescuing another soldier. The father was notified and grieved deeply for his only son.

About a month later, just before Christmas, there was a knock at the door. A young man stood at the door with a large package in his hands.

He said, "Sir, you don't know me, but I am the soldier for whom your son gave his life. He saved many lives that day, and he was carrying me to safety when a bullet struck him in the heart and he died instantly.

He often talked about you, and your love for art." The young man held out this package. "I know this isn't much. I'm not really a great artist, but I think your son would have wanted you to have this."

The father opened the package. It was a portrait of his son, painted by the young man. He stared in awe at the way the soldier had captured the personality of his son in the painting.

The father was so drawn to the eyes that his own eyes welled up with tears. He thanked the young man and offered to pay him for the picture. "Oh, no sir, I could never repay what your son did for me. It's a gift."

The father hung the portrait over his mantle. Every time visitors came to his home he took them to see the portrait of his son before he showed them any of the other great works he had collected.

The man died a few months later. There was to be a great auction of his paintings. Many influential people gathered, excited over seeing the great paintings and having an opportunity to purchase one for their collection.

On the platform sat the painting of the son. The auctioneer pounded his gavel. We will start the bidding with this picture of the son.

Who will bid for this picture?" There was silence.

Then a voice in the back of the room shouted, "We want to see the famous paintings. Skip this one."

But the auctioneer persisted. "Will someone bid for this painting? Who will start the bidding? $100, $200?" Another voice shouted angrily. We didn't come to see this painting. We came to see the Van Goghs, the Rembrandts. Get on with the real bids!"

But still the auctioneer continued. "The son! The son! Who'll take the son?"

Finally, a voice came from the very back of the room. It was the longtime gardener of the man and his son. "I'll give $10 for the painting." Being a poor man, it was all he could afford.

"We have $10, who will bid $20?"

"Give it to him for $10. Let's see the masters!" someone shouted.

"$10 is the bid, won't someone bid $20?"

The crowd was becoming angry. They didn't want the picture of the son. They wanted the more worthy investments for their collections.

The auctioneer pounded the gavel. "Going once, twice, SOLD for $10!"

A man sitting on the second row shouted, "Now let's get on with the collection!"

The auctioneer laid down his gavel. "I'm sorry, the auction is over."

"What about the paintings?"

"I am sorry. When I was called to conduct this auction, I was told of a secret stipulation in the will. I was not allowed to reveal that stipulation until this time. Only the painting of the son would be auctioned. Whoever bought that painting would inherit the entire estate, including the paintings. The man who took the son gets everything!"

God gave His son 2,000 years ago to die on a cruel cross.

Much like the auctioneer, His message today is: "The Son, the Son, who'll take the Son?" Because, you see, whoever takes the Son gets everything.

" He who has the Son has life; he who does not have the Son of God does not have life." - 1 John 5:12

—Author Unknown

Chapter 78

Three Hearts

Fill in the Blank:

1. There are hurt hearts, _____ hearts, and most important, _____ hearts.

2. The heart we hopefully yearn to know is the _____ heart.

3. God is more interested in what we do with a _____than with the hurt itself.

4. As we _____what is breaking our hearts, we are able to love freely again.

Discussion Questions:

1. What does the Bible say about "hardened" hearts? Support your answer with Scripture references.

2. The author writes, "God is more interested in what we do with a hurt than with the hurt itself." Why?

3. Which kind of heart should we want to have? Why?

4. According to the author, "Disobedience causes insecurity rather than security." Why is this true?

Group Activity:

Divide into three groups. Each group will be asked to take an assigned "heart" from this devotion and list as many characteristics as they can. Then discuss how the hurt heart and the hardened heart can become a liberating or forgiving heart. The group listing the characteristics of the liberating heart will also determine how to acquire these characteristics. Below is a start:

Hurt Heart	Hardened Heart	Liberating Heart
Anxiety	Withdrawn	Forgive others
Sadness	All advice is considered bad	Love others
Etc.	Etc.	Etc.

Digging Deeper:

Find a Scripture verse that talks about a hurt heart, hardened heart, and a liberating or forgiving heart.

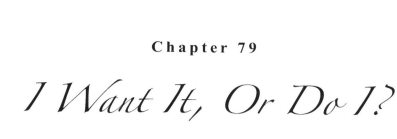

Chapter 79

I Want It, Or Do I?

Fill in the Blank:

1. Not striving to be _____ could mean we lack the desire to perform our _____ with integrity and heart.

2. It is time to explore the _____ challenge.

3. Attaining goals are accomplished by laying down _____, having a mind that continues to _____, and is being vulnerable to God.

4. One problem is _____ what someone else has.

Discussion Questions:

1. What is the difference in "wants" and "needs?" Give examples.

2. What is the mirror challenge?

3. The author says, "We are each a 'movement' in our personal timeline. What do you think the author means by this statement?

4. Why do you think coveting is such a problem? Explain.

Group Activity:

Ask someone to analyze Philippians 4:11-13 in relation to this devotional.

> Not that I speak in regard to need, for I have learned in whatever state I am, to be content: I know how to be abased, and I know how to abound. Everywhere and in all things I have learned both to be full and to be hungry, both to abound and to suffer need. I can do all things through Christ who strengthens me (NKJV).

Digging Deeper:

Find two more verses to go with the theme of this lesson—wanting what God wants us to have and not wanting what God does not want us to have.

Chapter 80

Attention Is Seasonal

Fill in the Blank:

1. It seems there is also _____ _____ when a church experiences growth.

2. A new church campus or enterprise needs extra _____ from time to time.

3. No one feels safe or _____ when experiencing an awkward stage of _____. Extra attention is what overcomes _____.

4. Whether you're a parent of a sibling during an awkward stage, or experiencing supernatural growth in your church or business, remember to give _____ _____ as needed.

Discussion Questions:

1. In the title to this devotion, the author says attention is seasonal. What do you think she means?

2. Why would there be rivalry when a church experiences growth? Explain.

3. How does extra attention overcome hurdles?

4. How did Paul show attention to the churches he planted during his missionary journeys?

Group Activity and Digging Deeper:

One might say that giving attention to sibling rivalries or the needs of a growing church could be likened to caring for people. In order for a church to be relevant, the people must be those who care for others. According to Dr. Paul Walker,* a caring church will find opportunities to care for one another. Some of the benefits are:

- It provides a sense of security and of belonging to something significant and purposeful.
- It makes the ministry vision relevant to everyday needs of people.
- It keeps people as the priority of ministry.

1. Considering these thoughts, can you think of ways to give attention to needs in the church and/or the community? Make suggestions.

2. What are some ways you have given attention to needs of others? Share a testimony with the class.

*Dr. Paul Walker is the pastor emeritus of the Mt. Paran Church of God in Atlanta, Georgia.

Chapter 81

Dig Deep and Uproot Those Weeds

Fill in the Blank:

1. Mowing the lawn made the yard look nice, but mowing alone won't get rid of _____.

2. You have to get down to the _____ of things.

3. We keep wearing what hides _____ while ignoring what we could do to _____ the underneath.

4. Without a strong _____, it is difficult for anything to last very long.

Discussion Questions:

1. How does the author compare her lawn to a spiritual walk with God?

2. How does one get down to the "root" of things, spiritually speaking?

3. Explain the author's additional comparison using clothes in paragraph four.

4. Explain the comparison of a tall building and its foundation to our spiritual condition.

Group Activity and Digging Deeper:

Ask the group to look at their spiritual heart as a flowerbed. Flowerbeds must be tended on a regular basis to keep out the weeds so the flowers and fruit can grow.

Stephen Colaw's sermon on "Cultivating Holiness: Cleaning Out the Weeds" states there are two kinds of weeds: One is recognizable and the other is misplaced weeds, which are not necessarily recognized as weeds.

*   Ask the group to read Galatians 5:19-21 and Colossians 3:5 and jot down the sins which are considered "weeds" in their flowerbed.

*   Ask the group to read Mark 10:17-23 and Luke 14:26-27 and identify what Jesus said sometimes becomes more important than our relationship with Him. These are things that

are misplaced and need to be moved to their proper places. (Also read Deuteronomy 5:7).

- When tending the garden of your heart, how do you know which things to eradicate and which things to move to their proper places? Why should we do this? (See Leviticus 11:44.)

- What flowers or fruit should be growing in your spiritual heart instead of weeds? Look up the scriptures that deal with the fruit of the Spirit.

- How do you recommend "tending" the garden of your heart?

Chapter 82

They ~ Them ~ Me

Fill in the Blank:

1. Prayer is not the "least we can do," rather, it's the _____.

2. Jesus is not _____ _____.

3. Delving into prayer for an enemy will definitely help you reach a _____ _____ in your prayer life.

4. A word spoken in _____ is the release and outpouring of _____ and God's best for mankind.

Discussion Questions:

1. What does the author say about the vague pronouns "they" and "them"?

2. What does she suggest as a personal question to ask? Do you agree?

3. What does the author suggest doing to help you reach a deeper level in one's prayer life? Is this what you do? Explain.

4. Answer the question: "Who am I?"

Group Activity:

Divide into small groups. Ask each group to go to Google and type in, "How to Become a Prayer Warrior." Browse through the selections. As a group, come up with a list of things to do to become a prayer warrior.

Ask the groups to share with the class what they came up with. Compare notes and discuss which things are the most important and workable for their own personal prayer lives.

Digging Deeper:

Read the Lord's Prayer found in Matthew 6:9-13. Someone has said that within the Lord's Prayer can be found a four-word "Prayer That Never Fails." Try to find it. (See the answer in the Answer Key to this chapter.)

Chapter 83

Inheritance

Fill in the Blank:

1. What I leave as an inheritance to my son is more than what can be _____ or _____.

2. By our mistakes, we are able to extend _____ as we teach our children, using _____ and diplomacy.

3. I try to use this recipe: _____, pray, acknowledge, _____, and repeat.

4. I am continually reminded there is no smaller window of _____ than with our _____.

Discussion Questions:

1. What kind of inheritance is the author referring to?

2. In the third paragraph, the author gives the reader a recipe that she follows. What is it?

3. How does this recipe work when leaving an inheritance to one's children?

4. The author uses a parable from Mark's Gospel to end her devotion. How does it tie in with the theme of inheritance? Explain

Group Activity:

For those in the group who have children, ask them to outline what they are doing to leave a spiritual inheritance for their children. Will this plan change as the children grow older? What are your projections?

For those who do not have children, ask them to reflect on their upbringing and what their parents did to prepare them for life? Would you do anything differently if you had children? Explain.

Digging Deeper:

Explain the differences in leaving a will for your heirs and leaving a spiritual heritage for them.

Find some scriptures that talk about heritage and write them down.

Chapter 84

Why Not Me?

Fill in the Blank:

1. God often speaks in the stillness of my _____ as I _____.

2. I stopped asking the pitiful question _____ . . . because God revealed to me the more pertinent question: _____?

3. _____ _____. It is the main possession the Enemy wants to steal from you.

4. We don't have to like _____, but it doesn't have to be our _____ either.

Discussion Questions:

1. Give an example of when you have asked God, "Why me?" Did you get an answer?

2. Do you think it is wrong to ask God, "Why me?" Explain.

3. How does God speak to you?

4. The author concludes the devotion with the following statement:

   "We don't have to like suffering, but it doesn't have to be our enemy either."

   What do you think this statement is telling us?

Group Activity:

Ask the group for volunteers to tell about a time when they went through a trial or a time of crisis. Answer the following questions as they relate their story:

- How did they react?

- What was the outcome?

- What lessons were learned?

Digging Deeper:

Find and write down scriptures that you think are helpful and comforting when going through a time of trial or crisis.

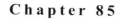

Chapter 85

Children Are a Bit Like
Time Capsules

Fill in the Blank:

1. The time capsule reveals an assortment of valuables from days past to the awaiting _____ _____. Sounds kind of like _____.

2. Our children are like _____ _____.

3. With what are we nourishing our children's _____ and _____?

4. Thinking of our children like a time capsule is a unique way to consider how we _____ them.

Discussion Questions:

1. The author uses a figure of speech (simile) to describe children. How does she weave this comparison throughout the devotion?

2. How does the author say she prepares her son for future life? How does this compare to what you do as parents, or how your parents prepared you?

3. If we are God's children, how is He preparing us for the future?

Group Activity Digging Deeper:

Divide into groups of husband/wife teams, or if no spouse, work as an individual.

Instructions for making a time capsule:

• Decide to use a mailing tube or a large padded envelope.

• Decide what you are going to put in your time capsule.

• Consider making the time capsule for yourself or your family.

- When will you open your time capsule? Five years from now? Ten years from now? Where will you hide it?

- Consider the following:

    —Write a letter to your future self in five or ten years.

    —Include items that are important to you at this time. When you open this capsule in five or ten years, you will find out if these things are still important to you.

    —What scripture verses are important to you at this time?

    —What do you perceive yourself doing for God in five or ten years?

    —Where do you think your children will be in five or ten years?

    —Where do you think the world will be in five or ten years from now?

- Date your time capsule and put the date it is to be opened in the future. Put it in its hiding place.

- Consider opening it sometime on New Year's Day. Do this every five or ten years. You might be amazed at where you are after five or ten years.

- If you have children old enough to do this exercise, you might want to help them construct and fill a time capsule of their own.

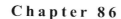

Chapter 86

Entitlement Cannot Unify

Fill in the Blank:

1. An entitlement _____ is a _____ in any situation no matter where it rises up.

2. An attitude of _____ lacks focus on righteous _____.

3. Family _____ is based on foundational _____ for one another.

4. I can't think of an instance where a _____ _____ is ever as important as a relationship between people.

Discussion Questions:

1. In your own words, explain entitlement.

2. Have you seen "entitlement" at work in a family or church situation? Share an example.

3. What is family unity based on? Explain how to avoid entitlement problems.

4. If selfishness is prevalent in a family member, how does one "undo" it?

Group Activity and Digging Deeper:

Divide into groups of two or three. Ask the groups to select one of the statements below and explain it. Do you know someone who fits into this category? Find a scripture or two that deals with this problem.

1. Like the alphabet, I comes before U.

2. What's yours is mine, and what's mine is my own.

3. Expectation of privilege is so great it leaves equality feeling like oppression.

4. An angry man/woman who feels his/her anger is justified.

5. "Poor little old me."

If time allows, ask someone from each group to share their scriptures for their selected problem.

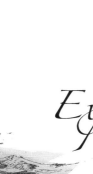

Chapter 87

Expect the Unexpected

Fill in the Blank:

1. Even the _____ is something God allows, because He certainly is not taken by _____.

2. In personal relationships, _____ _____ can hurt the deepest.

3. We are not to set anyone above our _____ with _____.

4. With God as your _____, stay prayed up in preparation for the _____.

Discussion Questions:

1. Give some examples of "unexpected" happenings in your life.

2. Give some examples of "unexpected" happenings in the Bible.

3. What are some possible solutions to help an individual be prepared for the unexpected?

4. The author gives her solution. What is it? Do you agree? Why?

Group Activity:

As a group, consider the unexpected scenarios below and offer suggestions how to be prepared for them. Find scriptures that deal with solving these problems in life.

1. Loss of a job due to no fault of your own, such as staff reduction, technology realignment, or company reorganization.

2. Death of a spouse or child.

3. Disability due to accident or sickness.

4. Teenage children who are causing unexpected problems, such as pregnancy, drugs, or running with the wrong crowd.

Digging Deeper:

Ask yourself how you are preparing for the unexpected. How are you answering the "What ifs?" in life? Example: What if I lost my job today? Could I support my family? Or myself? What if I became disabled? What would I do to survive until I could get disability started? How would I pay my bills?

Ruach: Spirit of God

Fill in the Blank:

1. The Hebrew word *Ruach* means, the "_____," like breath and _____.

2. God breathes life into us through _____, so that we can breathe life into others.

3. Embracing each day is like returning to our _____ _____, our passion, our _____, and our fire for life.

4. Don't settle on previous encounters with God that you continue to _____ about. Make _____ and _____ encounters as testimony.

Discussion Questions:

1. Can you think of instances in the Old Testament when the Spirit of God (*Ruach*—Hebrew word) was active? Discuss these with the group.

2. Can you think of instances in the New Testament when the Spirit of God was active? (In the New Testament Greek, the word is *pneuma*.) Discuss these instances with the group.

3. How can we have a fresh encounter with God? Explain.

4. Is it wrong to remember past encounters with God? Explain.

Group Activity and Digging Deeper:

As a group, using the Internet, a Bible concordance, etc., find as many instances as you can throughout the Bible describing the moving of the Spirit of God.

209 | *Ruach: Spirit of God*

Bible Reference	Name the Occasion	Describe the Benefit
Example: Genesis 1:1-2	Creation of the earth	God made the earth conducive for humans to live on.

Use extra paper if needed.

Chapter 89

The Tidy and Messy of It All

Fill in the Blank:

1. One of the meanings of being a visionary is to see beyond the _____.

2. I see the altar as a fully living, _____, functioning mainstay that reflects the heart and _____ of the church.

3. Whatever He (Jesus) did and wherever He went was consistently about the _____ _____.

4. _____ and _____ will always sort out what's "real."

Discussion Questions:

1. The author says the words "tidy" and "messy" have a powerful impact. What do you think she means?

2. How is being visionary important to the concept of "tidy and messy"? (Reread the first paragraph before answering.)

3. Explain the author's statement: "Relationship and time will always sort out what's real."

4. How important is our exterior looks when it comes to helping someone in need? Explain.

Group Activity and Digging Deeper:

The author makes the statement, "I see the altar as a fully living, biblical, and functioning mainstay that reflects the heart and vision of the church. One must experience the messy of digging deep to achieve full potential, glorifying God's kingdom."

Divide into two or three groups. Ask the groups to discuss the above statements, making sure they understand the implications referring to the altar.

Find at least two scripture references in the Bible where the altar was a fully living and functioning mainstay. Explain the biblical references you chose to the rest of the group, and explain how your choice "glorifies God's kingdom."

Chapter 90

Sadducees and Pharisees

Fill in the Blank:

1. They (Sadducees and Pharisees) resolved to do their utmost to _____ ____ _____ of who Jesus was.

2. The act of seeking and following Christ is not _____ by the unveiling of oneself either in _____ or vulnerability.

3. Achieving _____ is an open book course of action—one that we will continue while here on earth, page after page.

4. As the most broken of broken people are tended to with _____, they begin to see themselves for the first time as Christ sees them.

Discussion Questions:

1. The author begins this devotion by saying, "Sadducees and Pharisees weren't big on anyone other than themselves." Which Bible scriptures verify this statement?

2. Why did the Sadducees and Pharisees try to "remove the truth of who Jesus was"?

3. Explain the author's statement: "Achieving Christlikeness is an open book course of action."

4. The author declares that "when broken people are tended with compassion, they begin to see themselves as Christ sees them." Why is this statement a beautiful hope?

Group Activity and Digging Deeper:

Pair off into groups of two. Using the Internet and their Bibles, the pairs should research what the differences and likenesses are between the Sadducees and Pharisees. Make a chart with the following headings:

Sadducees	Pharisees	Internet Site	Biblical Reference
Did not believe in angels or Resurrection	Believed in angels and the Resurrection	Differences in ……..	Acts 23:8

Chapter 91

May I Serve You?

Fill in the Blank:

1. _____ is an issue when people are in a vulnerable state.

2. For those uncomfortable on the receiving end of assistance, it is their _____ to experience what it's like to be known on a deeper level.

3. For those uncomfortable with reaching out, they are experiencing what it's like to touch another's life in a _____ and _____ way.

4. _____ serve others and _____ accept being served. It's God's way.

Discussion Questions:

1. The author says, when someone asks: "'How may I serve you?' they are allowing you into a region of insecurity." Explain this statement.

2. The author says a "miraculous change" occurs in the person serving another. What kind of change is taking place? Why does change occur?

3. Which professions are considered "service-oriented"? Are churches and those who work in the church considered to be in a "service-oriented" profession? How so?

4. In Luke 10, Jesus relates a story about someone who was "service-oriented." Explain how this story exemplifies "service" to another? There is an opposite viewpoint in the same story. What is the irony involved here?

5. The author relates a personal experience her family went through and how it influenced everyone in the family. Has your family had such an experience? Please share your experience with the group.

Group Activity:

Ask the group to go to the Internet and research "service-oriented" professions. Make a list of as many as they can find. How varied are they? Why are some professions like software development considered "service-oriented?" What other professions are listed in this category that surprised you? Why?

Digging Deeper:

Find three scriptures related to serving others.

Chapter 92

Stepping Stones

Fill in the Blank:

1. Stepping stones serve a _____. They are to be stepped _____, not _____.

2. _____ a stepping stone can be the very thing you needed _____ to miss.

3. We should all consider _____we are going, _____ we want to get there, and _____ preparation is required.

4. When we do our best and strive for excellence, our journey will be as it's supposed to be: _____ _____.

Discussion Questions:

1. What is the purpose of stepping stones?
   A. What is their purpose physically?
   B. What is their purpose spiritually?

2. What might be the consequences if a stepping stone (or building block) is skipped?

3. What is the difference in going from Point A to Point B if one hurries by the shortest route or goes slowly by a leisurely route? Is this difference important? Why?

4. Why is order important to God?

Group Activity and Digging Deeper:

Divide into two or three groups. Have them select an activity from the ones suggested below:

1. Find examples in the Bible where Jesus used organizational skills. Share with the group.

2. Solomon in the Book of Proverbs talks about the ant. How is the ant organized? Are there patterns in their work? What lessons can we learn from the ant? Share your findings with the group.

3. Read 2 Timothy 2:15. What does this scripture say about living our lives in an organized manner so that there will be "no regrets." Explain this scripture to the group with an example.

Chapter 93

Me and My Shadow

Fill in the Blank:

1. _____ is as close to me as my shadow.

2. Nothing could keep Him (Christ) away from His _____ and destiny of permanently _____ us.

3. He (Christ) does hear our cries for _____ and knows our surrender when we reach our _____ _____.

4. It is important to remember that we are never too far out of His _____, and His _____ have always been upon us.

Discussion Questions:

1. Explain the figure of speech (simile) in the second sentence of this devotion.

2. Explain the spiritual implications in the last sentence of the first paragraph.

3. At the end of this devotion, the author uses Psalm 23 as a supporting scripture. Why do you think she chose this passage as support for this devotion?

4. In the very last sentence of this devotion, the author says, "My life is an unfolding story of me and my shadow." What does she mean? Who is her shadow?

Group Activity and Digging Deeper:

Ask someone in the group to read Psalm 23:4. Now ask the group to answer the following questions:

1. What does the "valley" represent?

2. Is the valley dark? Justify your answer.

3. Someone once said in order to have a shadow, there must be a light. If this is true, then where is the light coming from?

4. The last part of this verse says, "I will fear no evil; for You are with me." Who is "You"?

5. Now, ask someone in the group to explain the entire verse. How is this verse hopeful to the Christian?

Chapter 94

What's Your Modus Operandi?

Fill in the Blank:

1. If we have the wrong _____, then our reaction or response will be _____ also.

2. Much of what we evaluate is based on something _____.

3. It is an astonishing journey—this taking an _____ look—but, the rewards are _____ because of the depth and difficulty of the trek.

4. It is not only _____ we think, but it is also _____ we think.

Discussion Questions:

1. The author says we are all flawed. Do you agree? Explain your answer.

2. When we are upset, the author suggests that we should look inwardly. Why?

3. The author quotes someone as saying, "The very thing which is irritating to me is also inside me." Do you agree with this statement? If this is true, then what can be done about the situation?

4. Have you had a soul-searching journey? If so, perhaps you could share it with the group.

Group Activity:

Ask the group to read the following quote taken from the Internet.

"Life is like a sandwich!
      Birth as one slice,
      and death as the other.
      What you put in-between
      the slices is up to you.

Is your sandwich tasty or sour?"
                              —**Allan Rufus**

Ask the group to discuss this quote and offer their opinion of the analogy. Is it true? Are we responsible for what makes up our lives?

Digging Deeper:

How does one search his own soul? David asked God to search his soul in Psalm 139:23. So, is it a combination of God and the individual searching one's soul? What are your thoughts?

Chapter 95

There Are No Stupid Questions

Fill in the Blank:

1. What we don't know should never hold us back; it should be the determining _____ causing us to press on and _____ as an apprentice would.

2. There is _____ in being able to inquire.

3. Things to learn from life experiences:

   A. Know who you are in _____.
   B. Be able to always _____ _____ on the inside.
   C. _____ those who persecute you.

4. I have learned to _____ the most contrary and problematic people and situations because they taught me the _____.

Discussion Questions:

1. The title to this devotion says, "There Are No Stupid Questions." Do you agree? What do you consider a "stupid question"?

2. The author says there is "freedom" in being able to inquire. Why is this statement true?

3. Have you ever had to face the individual who was persecuting or bullying you? How did you react facing that person? What was the outcome?

4. The author says she has learned to embrace the difficult situations in life, because they taught her the most. What does one learn from these kinds of situations in life? Have you found this to be true? Give an example.

Group Activity:

Ask someone in the group to read aloud Psalm 119:71 (used as a support verse for this devotion). Discuss this verse as a group.

- What do we learn from affliction? Give an example.

- What are the "statutes" that we are to learn from affliction?

- Why is affliction conducive to learning?

Has anyone in the group experienced learning from affliction? If so, could they share the experience?

Digging Deeper:

Read 2 Chronicles 33:10-13 as an example of learning from affliction.

Chapter 96

Remember

Fill in the Blank:

1. The harder we try to forget something, the more we _____ it.

2. The act of _____ releases us to receive what God has for us.

3. We are reminded of the _____ that Christ must have endured for each and every one of us. God doesn't want us to _____ that.

4. In all of humanity, the _____ is where our deepest _____ is birthed.

Discussion Questions:

1. The author begins her devotion by saying, "The harder we try to forget something, the more we remember it." Is this true? Give an example.

2. Who benefits from an act of forgiveness—the person forgiving, the one being forgiven, or both? Explain.

3. What does God not want us to forget? Why? What are the consequences if we do?

4. What is it about the cross that causes us to have deep compassion? Explain.

Group Activity:

Ask three group members to select one of the three verses at the end of this devotion and read it aloud. The verses deal with remembrance and forgiveness, with Jesus being our example. Why, in your opinion, should Christians take Communion? How does it benefit the believer? What are the consequences if we don't take Communion? What are the consequences if we don't forgive those who have wronged us? Can anyone share an example of the consequences of unforgiveness?

Digging Deeper:

Look up at least three more verses dealing with remembrance.

Chapter 97

Denial Is Not a Good Hiding Place

Fill in the Blank:

1. In response to a direct question, _____ can still be a lie.

2. The roots of _____ run deep, being birthed in deceit.

3. Facing what I know to be _____ to me is painful.

4. _____ Christ seems like _____ to both our physical and spiritual wellbeing.

Discussion Questions:

1. Explain the title of this devotion.

2. According to the author, "silence can still be a lie." Explain this statement and give an example.

3. The author uses a simile (figure of speech) of an onion when attempting to find the truth. Explain this simile.

4. Explain this statement: "Rejecting Christ seems like betrayal to both our physical and spiritual wellbeing." Why is rejection a betrayal to the physical wellbeing?

Group Activity and Digging Deeper:

Ask the group to answer the following questions about lying and denial:

1. At what point does the omission of truth become a lie? Give an example.

2. At the Last Supper, Judas Iscariot was silent when Jesus said someone would betray him. He simply got up from the table and left. Was this lying?

3. At the Last Supper, Peter vehemently protested against the statement that he would deny Jesus. Was he intentionally lying? Did this expose his inner self? At the trial, why did the accusers not believe Peter's denial?

4. What is this devotion telling us?

5. How does Luke 8:17 apply to this devotion?

Chapter 98

Throw Down the Gauntlet

Fill in the Blank:

1. Enemies, like bullies, antagonize and _____us in order to show our weakness or more likely, make us believe we are _____and _____.

2. When we "throw down the gauntlet" or glove, it means a desire to _____ or _____ another.

3. We will continue to be _____ by someone else's behavior or ideas; therefore, we need to _____ for what's right.

4. Like soldiers in pursuit of victory, we can _____ _____ opposing forces or _____ over them right here and right now while on earth.

Discussion Questions:

1. In the first paragraph, the author uses a figure of speech about Achilles' heel. Explain the metaphor and how it is used.

2. The author uses a second metaphor in the second paragraph about throwing down the gauntlet. She explains how she is using this metaphor. Do you agree? Give an example.

3. Explain the simile in the last paragraph: "Like soldiers in pursuit of victory, we can push back opposing forces or trample over them." Does this mean we literally trample people? Give an example of how believers in Christ can exemplify this simile.

Group Activity:

Ask the group the following question: Why do you think the Bible (both Old and New Testaments) uses war imagery? Give several reasons backed with Bible references.

The New Testament even uses the imagery of a Christian soldier dressed in battle armor. (Find the passage and read it aloud.) Explain the pieces of the armor and how this imagery can be used today for the believer.

Digging Deeper:

Dress the modern Christian soldier in 21st –century war attire. What does he look like? Are we still battling our Enemy in the same way? Explain.

Chapter 99

Loving God Is a Dynamic Force

Fill in the Blank:

1. The dynamic force of loving _____ and what He loves is the sustenance and _____ that motivate me.

2. The voice of _____ is a confidence that brings _____ of what's coming.

3. We can never _____ too much if we love with the _____ of God's Word.

4. Life is a great deal more _____ when we make it more about _____ of others rather than a sought-after, _____ social standing.

Discussion Questions:

1. In the first paragraph, the author refers to the dynamic force of God's breath when He breathes on believers. What happens when God breathes on mankind? Use scripture to support your answer.

2. In the Book of Acts, the disciples became "voices of authority." What dynamic force changed them? Explain, using Scripture.

3. The author says we can "never love too much . . ." Read paragraph three and decide whether you agree. There have been cases where someone loved another person deeply, and then they turned on them and betrayed them. How do you explain this? How should a believer in this case respond?

Group Activity:

Ask someone in the group to read paragraph four aloud. Ask for examples of what the author is saying in paragraph four. Sometimes, people today do not want to be helped. How does the Christian respond? Give examples.

Digging Deeper:

Read each of the Scripture passages at the end of this devotion (p. 204). Determine what the predominant theme is for each of them.

Imagine Doing What You've Only Imagined

Fill in the Blank:

1. This journey is more than you've _____.

2. Imagine something that requires yet something more: _____.

3. I think how we travel the journey _____ _____.

4. We collect memories along our trek, enabling us to _____ a picture with _____ for our children and grandchildren.

Discussion Questions:

1. Are daydreams ever actually realized? Explain and give an example.

2. The author says how we travel the journey "matters greatly." Why? Explain.

3. The author says, "If you've never thought of how you sow, now is a good time to start." What does this mean? How do you sow?

4. The theme of sowing and reaping is touched on in paragraph two. The theme of leaving a legacy is touched on in paragraph four. Do the two go together? Explain.

Group Activity:

Go around the group and ask each person what he or she imagined as a child they would do when they grew up. Did that "dream" materialize? If not, what changed their dream? Psalm 37:23 says, "The steps of a good man are ordered by the Lord" (NKJV). Can you see how God ordered your steps and your dreams?

Digging Deeper (For Individual Perusal):

How are you sowing and reaping? What legacy are you planning to leave your family?

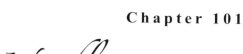

Chapter 101

Needless Extra Baggage

Fill in the Blank:

1. How do we avoid clutter? Speaking from a spiritual viewpoint, I say: "Lord, _____ _____."

2. Let go of things like _____ of the past, hurts, offenses, and _____. _____ is not yours to repay; God will contend with them.

3. It is important for Christians to _____ and care for God's people by providing spiritual _____ from the young to the _____.

4. Trade in your burdens for _____, preparing yourself to better _____ new things from God.

Discussion Questions:

1. What is some of the baggage Christians carry around?

2. How do we get rid of the extra baggage? Give scripture references in your answer.

3. If we suddenly find ourselves with more to do than we can properly take care of, what does the Bible say to do? Give a Bible reference for your answer.

Group Activity:

Ask the group how important it is for believers to rest. What are some suggestions for being able to rest, especially with our busy lifestyles today? Write down the suggestions and keep them for future use.

Digging Deeper:

Find at least two verses in the New Testament that talk about rest.

Chapter 102

Unlocking Your Kairos Moments

Fill in the Blank:

1. What takes place verbally in _____ sets the platform for _____ and connecting something that cannot and should not be broken.

2. Conversation is a healthy way to establish an _____ _____ policy with others.

3. It is the simplicity of _____ and _____ coming together that builds a healthy _____.

Discussion Questions:

1. What is the best way to unlock a Kairos Moment? Why?

2. The author says verbal conversation "sets the platform for building and connecting something that cannot and should not be broken." What is this "something" she is referring to? Do you agree? Why?

3. How do we build a healthy future?

4. Would this suggestion work in our society today? Justify your answer.

Group Activity:

Ask each person to take out a sheet of paper (or give each person a piece of paper) and ask him or her to evaluate this book by answering the following questions.

1. List at least three things (more if you want to) you learned from this book.

2. What would you suggest doing to make the book better?

3. Has this workbook been helpful?
   • Have the Discussion Questions made you think when answering?
   • Have you learned from the group activities and by interacting with others?
   • Did you complete the "Digging Deeper" activity? Why or why not?

4. What is a Kairos Moment?

5. Turn in the evaluation sheet to the facilitator.

Chapter 103

Dream Your Dreams

Fill in the Blank:

1. Simplify your _____.

2. The facts say one _____; your heart says _____.

3. I believe Your favor is _____on me.

4. Cease telling God and others why dreams _____ _____.

Discussion Questions:

1. Why do facts and dreams at times conflict?

2. How do you know if your dream is from God or if you just think you want to do this?

3. Should we pray for our dreams to come true?

Group Activity:

Have someone read 1 Chronicles 4:10 aloud.

Ask the group to contribute their thoughts (negative and positive) about the Prayer of Jabez.

Are we being selfish when we ask God to increase our territory?

Should we ask God to bless us? Or, is this something that comes with right living?

Have you ever asked God to keep you from causing pain to another?

Digging Deeper:

Look up several prayers in the Bible. Which is your favorite? Why?

Answer Key

Fill in the blank questions

WORKBOOK ANSWER KEY
FILL IN THE BLANKS

Chapter 1:
1. Offense; abuse; criticism
2. Forgiving
3. Potter's wheel
4. Miraculous; immediate
5. Process

Chapter 2:
1. Christ; can be done in me
2. Beginning of something new
3. "Throwaways"
4. Can resurface

Chapter 3:
1. Opportunities
2. Modus operandi
3. Marred future
4. God's view

Chapter 4:
1. Healthy relationships
2. The Word
3. Almanac
4. Accountability

Chapter 5:
1. Visually; faith
2. One's best
3. Mistakes
4. Faith

Chapter 6:
1. Domestic engineering; stay-at-home mom
2. Opportunity
3. Tired
4. Children

Chapter 7:
1. Freedom
2. Hearing the Word; action
3. Gifts
4. Utilize; freedom

Chapter 8:
1. New life
2. Revitalizes
3. Rest
4. Dead things; new healthy growth

Chapter 9:
1. Irritates
2. Dominion
3. Brothers and sisters; dominion
4. Forbearance

Chapter 10:
1. Purpose
2. Personalities; characteristics
3. Complement
4. Stagnant

Chapter 11:
1. Praise; adoration
2. Goodness; liberation
3. Standards
4. Fruit of the Spirit

Chapter 12:
1. Word
2. Trust; faith
3. Iron
4. Discernment
5. Resistance

Chapter 13:
1. Bless
2. Dignity; respect
3. Behavior
4. Godliness

Chapter 14:
1. Circumstances; surroundings
2. Breath Prayer
3. Scope of prayer
4. Underestimated

Chapter 15:
1. Responsibility; consequences
2. Plain view
3. Humility
4. Junctures

Chapter 16:
1. Beneficial
2. Heart of God
3. Craving
4. Hearts and minds

Chapter 17:
1. Time
2. Gone forever
3. Manage
4. Liberated

Chapter 18:
1. Planned
2. Listen
3. Best friend
4. Prayer

Chapter 19:
1. His
2. Burdens
3. Exchange
4. Promises

Chapter 20:
1. Tone of voice
2. Others; us
3. Thoughts
4. Inspirational

Chapter 21:
1. Roots
2. Underground; above
3. Wind
4. Flexibility

Chapter 22:
1. Unexpected
2. Upsets
3. Stewardship
4. Questioning; individualism

Chapter 23:
1. People
2. Hurt
3. People watching
4. Criticism

Chapter 24:
1. Goodness
2. Often; authority
3. Internet
4. Bring forth

Chapter 25:
1. With
2. Catapult
3. Steps of faith
4. Onward

Chapter 26:
1. Advantageous
2. Tomorrow
3. Producers
4. Father's business

Chapter 27:
1. Omnipotent
2. Pride
3. Pride
4. Words spoken

Chapter 28:
1. Peace
2. Concentrate
3. Grateful
4. Others; tolerable

Chapter 29:
1. Individually
2. Change
3. Turbulence
4. New; profound

Chapter 30:
1. Communication
2. Full-time job
3. Balance problem
4. Platter; hand of God

Chapter 31:
1. Investment
2. Patience
3. Hope
4. Choice

Chapter 32:
1. Thinking
2. Altar
3. Promises
4. Beauty for ashes

Chapter 33:
1. Miles upon miles
2. Granted
3. Has; is; continues
4. Physical

Chapter 34:
1. Boundaries
2. Communicative
3. Authority; responsibilities
4. God; provider

Chapter 35:
1. Knowledge
2. Wisdom
3. Acuity
4. Implement

Chapter 36:
1. Large gaps
2. Thread; freely
3. Tension
4. Daily

Chapter 37:
1. Treat others
2. Empty; striving
3. Lifestyle
4. Comparison

Chapter 38:
1. Traveling
2. Creative
3. Body; mind; spirit
4. Preparation

Chapter 39:
1. Clearly; biblically; honestly
2. Truth
3. Mirror
4. Pride; godly

Chapter 40:
1. Emotions
2. Vulnerable; timid
3. Clarity
4. Way; way

Chapter 41:
1. Safety
2. Prepare
3. Inside; surface
4. Direction; slip

Chapter 42:
1. Encounter
2. Masked
3. Paradigm
4. Revealed

Chapter 43:
1. Powerful; defies
2. Straightforward
3. Noticed
4. Small; manage

Chapter 44:
1. Destiny; object
2. Fantastic; endless
3. Light; travels
4. Light

Chapter 45:
1. Continuously
2. Remnant
3. Word of God
4. One

Chapter 46:
1. Eye; beholder
2. Appearance; deeper
3. Commandment
4. Self-portrait

Chapter 47:
1. Anything; excursion
2. Embrace
3. Risky
4. Fearful; ready

Chapter 48:
1. Vision
2. Visionless; hopeless
3. Sever
4. Pure heart

Chapter 49:
1. Territory
2. Water
3. Jericho
4. Motivated; add on

Chapter 50:
1. Cheating; intellect
2. Spoke; understood
3. Maturing; adult
4. Creative

Chapter 51:
1. Astray; abandon
2. Strengthen; shelter
3. Pathway
4. Question; opinion

Chapter 52:
1. Compilation; history
2. Inaccuracies; waste
3. Begin
4. Prevents; anguish

Chapter 53:
1. Anticipation; urgency
2. Commandment
3. Love; wildfire
4. Catalyst; truth

Chapter 54:
1. Eyes; protect
2. Preparation
3. Understand; ourselves
4. Voice; God

Chapter 55:
1. Wonders; enthusiasm
2. Personality; consistent
3. Yesterday; today
4. Most High

Chapter 56:
1. Maze; through
2. Correct; benefit
3. Restoring; undeniable
4. Right; wrong.

Chapter 57:
1. Transcends
2. Creative; connect
3. Relationship
4. God

Chapter 58:
1. Offended; maturity
2. Behavior
3. Humble; approachable
4. Mistakes

Chapter 59:
1. Obvious; bombarded
2. Endurance
3. Reason; season
4. Motion; aspects

Chapter 60:
1. Nourished
2. Deface; people
3. Awakening; regimen
4. Downhill; course

Chapter 61:
1. Participation
2. Belong
3. Children; bond
4. Adversities; conquer

Chapter 62:
1. Downtrodden fresh air
2. Refreshing; refreshed
3. Paul; attitudes
4. Important; therapy

Chapter 63:
1. Obedience; fear
2. Fear; reject
3. Overcome; wisdom
4. Temptation

Chapter 64:
1. Human race
2. Wayward
3. Disciples; Jesus
4. Decaying; hands; feet

Chapter 65:
1. Loved ones; front door
2. Physical; heart
3. "Loved one"; love
4. Path

Chapter 66:
1. Fear; strength
2. God
3. Scrutinize; necessary
4. Feats

Chapter 67:
1. Politeness; wayside
2. Wants
3. Apology; excuse
5. Other person

Chapter 68:
1. Youngsters
2. Skills; occurrences
3. Fragile; wind
4. Nurture; shipping

Chapter 69:
1. Procrastination
2. Delay; positive
3. Regret; procrastination
4. Authorizes; responsible

Chapter 70:
1. Good
2. Bad habit; standstill
3. Personal; humility
4. Love; truth

Chapter 71:
1. Discernment
2. Comes to visit
3. Guilt; condemnation
4. Listening; taught

Chapter 72:
1. Inner beauty; outer
2. Inside
3. Change; transformation
4. Transformation; changed

Chapter 73:
1. Belief; doubt
2. Apprehension; possibilities
3. Victorious
4. Doubt; credence

Chapter 74:
1. Lazy
2. Scheduling
3. Iron; iron
4. Personality

Chapter 75:
1. Emotion; high
2. Faultfindings; harm; unforgiveness
3. Kind; validation
4. Opposite

Chapter 76:
1. Convene
2. Quiet time
3. Significance; chaos
4. Excellence

Chapter 77:
1. Reflection
2. Essential; proliferate
3. Potter
4. Original

Chapter 78:
1. Hardened; liberated
2. Liberating
3. Hurt
4. Liberate

Chapter 79:
1. Reliable; responsibilities
2. Mirror
3. Pride; learn
4. Coveting

Chapter 80:
1. Sibling rivalry
2. Attention
3. Adequate; growth; hurdles
4. Seasonal attention

Chapter 81:
1. Weeds
2. Root
3. Imperfections; improve
4. Foundation

Chapter 82:
1. Best we can do
2. Past tense
3. Deeper level
4. Prayer; hope
Digging Deeper Answer:
"Thy will be done" (Matthew 6:10b).

Chapter 83:
1. Bought; sold
2. Grace; wisdom
3. Praise; thanks
4. Time; children

Chapter 84:
1. Heart; listen
2. Why me? Why not you?
3. Simple joy
4. Suffering; enemy

Chapter 85:
1. Future audience; faith
2. Time capsules
3. Bodies; minds
4. Train

Chapter 86:
1. Attitude; wedge
2. Entitlement; behavior
3. Unity; love
4. Material object

Chapter 87:
1. Unexpected; surprise
2. Unplanned situations
3. Relationship; Christ
4. Standard; unexpected

Chapter 88:
1. Spirit of God; wind
2. Scripture
3. First love; desire
4. Testify; new; fresh

Chapter 89:
1. Superficial
2. Biblical; vision
3. Father's business
4. Relationship; time

Chapter 90:
1. Remove the truth
2. Intimidated; transparency
3. Christlikeness
4. Compassion

Chapter 91:
1. Trust
2. Awakening
3. Personal; positive
4. Humbly; humbly

Chapter 92:
1. Purpose; upon; over
2. Skipping; not
3. Where; how; what
4. No regrets

Chapter 93:
1. Christ
2. Purpose; adopting
3. Help; wits end
4. Reach; eyes

Chapter 94:
1. Reasoning; askew
2. Deeper
3. Inward; remarkable
4. What; how

Chapter 95:
1. Factor; absorb
2. Freedom
3. Christ; stand up; face
4. Embrace; most

Chapter 96:
1. Remember
2. Forgiving
3. Pain; forget
4. Cross; compassion

Chapter 97:
1. Silence
2. Betrayal
3. Harmful
4. Rejecting; betrayal

Chapter 98:
1. Dare; pitiful; scrawny
2. Challenge; confront
3. Challenged; stand up
4. Push back; trample

Chapter 99:
1. God; guide
2. Authority; awareness
3. Love; purity
4. Gratifying; needs; self-serving

Chapter 101:
1. Purify me
2. Ugliness; wrongdoings; vengeance
3. Tend; food; fully mature
4. Rest; receive

Chapter 103:
1. Thoughts
2. Thing; another
3. Resting
4. Can't happen

Chapter 100:
1. Envisioned
2. Action
3. Matters greatly
4. Paint; stories

Chapter 102:
1. Relationship; building
2. Open door
3. Action; words; future

Made in the USA
Columbia, SC
14 January 2022

54221725R00137